This Side of Crazy

This Side of Crazy

LESSONS ON LIVING
FROM SOMEONE
WHO SHOULD KNOW BETTER
BUT KEEPS MESSING UP ANYWAY

Allen Johnson, Ph.D.

RENAISSANCE PUBLISHING HOUSE
Richland, Washington

ISBN: 0-9626600-0-0

Library of Congress Catalog Card Number: 90-91711

Printed in the United States of America.

FOR **Nita**

ACKNOWLEDGEMENTS

My thanks to Doris Lisk, Mary Alice Hawkins, Pat Means, and Judy Clem for their friendship and admirable editing and proofreading skills. My appreciation, also, to the *Tri-City Herald,* where most of these stories first appeared.

INTRODUCTION

THIS SIDE OF CRAZY is where you want to be.
It is the side of reason, maturity, and emotional
stability. It is also the place where you collect
more laughs and fewer bellyaches. When you are
able to say "I'm okay" and willing to see virtue in
others, you are standing on "This Side of Crazy."
When you can unclog the kitchen sink without
unraveling or accept unconditionally the contour of
your nose or resist the temptation to submit, oh so
sweetly, "That nitwit is missing a few buttons!" —
when you can manage to accomplish all that, you
have joined the forces on "This Side of Crazy."

But what does it take to get there? The essays
compiled in this collection offer some hints. For
the most part the stories are drawn from personal
experiences, not because I have achieved perfection
— not in *this* lifetime — but because I was always

present when the stuff happened.

I believe in being real. I think that is the only way to make contact with people. So I have written as truthfully as I know how, without a lot of glitz or pretense. I hope that we become friends through these words and phrases. I don't see how we could do otherwise; my aim was to write from the heart.

The thoughts that I have shared in these pages have been helpful to me. They are principles that I strive to live by. I believe they are ideas that promote personal integrity, interpersonal depth, and the elixir to life's toughest battles, good humor. I hope a few of them make sense to you and help you in your quest to rest safely on "This Side of Crazy."

Yours by Choice
Allen Johnson

This Side of Crazy

LAST NIGHT I SLEPT UNDER THE STARS. The newspaper reported there would be a spectacular comet shower, an event that happens only once a year. So, I got out my sleeping bag and favorite pillow and pitched camp in my back yard.

My old English sheepdog settled down beside me. He stared at me, his head cocked and eyebrows raised in wonder.

"How unexpected and doglike," he must have thought.

The sky was clear; the air was cool. It was a perfect night for stargazing. With every falling star, I felt a small jolt, a gentle leap of joy. Soon I began thinking about another night under the stars long ago, the night I met the girl who broke my heart.

I was fourteen years old. My family was

spending the summer at Newman Lake northeast of
Spokane. It was the perfect setting for a summer
romance — mountains, trees, beach, and water.

One night, my brother, a friend, and I walked
to a nearby coffee shop at Honeymoon Bay Resort
to play the pinball machines. That's when I saw
her — a beautiful, platinum blond, fourteen-year-
old woman of the world. I knew she was
experienced; she had that serene look of carnal
knowledge.

"Who is *that*?" I asked my friend, pointing with
the side of my head, so as not to be conspicuous.

"That's Julie," my friend said. "Forget her.
She goes with the paper boy, and he's sixteen."

But evidently Julie felt no bond of loyalty to
the young journalist. She walked directly to me
and introduced herself.

"Hi, my name is Julie."

Boy, was she smooth.

Then she did something I'll never forget. She
playfully stepped on my brand new, low-cut tennis
shoes; it was so cool.

That was the beginning of the romance of the
summer. We spent every day together —
swimming, water skiing, sun bathing. At night we

looked at the stars and kissed a lot; it's amazing how long two fourteen-year-olds can kiss.

And then it happened. One morning near the end of the summer, I looked out our cabin window that overlooked the lake. I was killed. There were Julie and the sixteen-year-old paper boy, scuba diving off the end of the dock. A few moments later they were driving off together in his '58 Chevy convertible.

That was the end. There was no goodbye — nothing. The summer was over, and I started another year at school. But all year long I thought about Julie. At night, I lay in bed with my eyes open and made up stories about what happened. I imagined that she was kidnapped and drugged and sold to an Arab prince in the white slave market. That was the only possible explanation.

It was two years before I saw Julie again. We were spending another summer at the lake. Julie was there and even prettier than I had remembered. I did not speak to her; I was too nervous. But she spoke to me. One evening she asked if I would like to go for a walk — as if anything could stop me.

We strolled silently to a nearby picnic area. I leaned against a large pine, both hands tucked into my back pockets, trying to look as tragic as possible.

I rehearsed the familiar words in my head. "Julie," I finally said, "what happened two summers ago?"

She looked at me sadly. "Oh, Allen," she whispered, "I was so immature. And you are so neat, the sweetest guy I've ever known. How could I have left you? Can you ever forgive me?"

Then she stepped forward and pressed her lips against mine. I was transported to heaven. For a moment I think I lost control of my bladder. It was better than all of my fantasies.

Again, the romance rekindled—no, inflamed. By the end of the summer, we were totally devoted. We promised each other that we would write faithfully and reunite the following summer.

Every week I wrote to Julie, spicing my letters with lines of poetry from my freshman literature book. And then I did something that was outrageously stupid.

I had been raised in a very conservative church. We were taught that there were many worldly things to tempt us—all of which should be carefully avoided. One of those vices was going to the movies; Christians did not do that.

Yet Julie, who called herself a Christian, *did*
go. How was that possible? I was deeply troubled
by the paradox, so I challenged her in a letter.

I waited a week for her response; there was
none. I waited two weeks; still no response.
Finally, I realized what I had done. I quickly wrote
another letter.

"Who am I to judge you?" I wrote. "Please
forgive me."

I mailed the letter and waited. A week went
by, two weeks, a month. Julie never wrote again.
And I was sick with remorse and shame.

Years later, after I had graduated from college,
I decided to give Julie a call. I wanted to know
what had happened to her; I wondered if she was
happy. But mostly, I wanted to reminisce, to share
some of the old stories, to think back for a few
moments on the thrill of young love.

Julie answered the phone, and I introduced
myself. Immediately, I felt a coolness, a distancing
from me. There was no common bond. Julie had
no desire to reminisce. She assured me quickly,
and very politely, that she was happily married; in
fact, life could not be better.

"You do not understand," I wanted to say. "I do not want to break up your marriage; I only want to remember."

That may have been the saddest phone call I've ever made.

Last night, I thought about all that while watching the shooting stars. Awed by the magnitude of the universe, I marvelled at my audacity. How could I, a speck in time and space, ever have thought I could sit in for God?

IT IS FRIDAY NIGHT, the day of the big game. The high school gym is pulsating, a sneeze away from cardiac thrombosis. Wearing our home whites, we explode onto the court. The first layup drill is flawless: basketball choreography.

The cheerleaders, with their cute little skirts and terminal enthusiasm, are burning 500 calories a minute. They love us: "ALLEN, ALLEN, HE'S OUR MAN; IF HE CAN'T DO IT, NO ONE CAN!"

I played in the band.

I must have played at a hundred games. And in all that time not one cheerleader ever shouted, "Allen, Allen, he's our man; if he can't toot it, no one can." Ooooh, no. They'd scream their buns off for a six-foot-four flagpole in boxer shorts. But a trumpet player never got boo.

Am I bitter? Yes. Am I jealous? You bet. Do I want restitution? You're darn tootin'.

The problem is my athletic career peaked in the sixth grade. That was the year I was all-play-ground, the fastest kid at Emerson Elementary. I ran so fast my sneakers wheezed.

But that supremacy was short-lived. In the seventh grade one or two kids with sprouts of hair on their chests could nose me out in a sprint. In the eighth grade there were a few more. By the time I was a senior in high school, my great aunt, Boxcar Thelma, could whip me. I don't know what happened; all my fast-twitch muscles suddenly went limp.

Oh, I'm not really bitter; I'm more envious than anything else. You see, the thing that I admire about athletes—the ones who really understand the meaning of teamwork—is how they support each other: cheering the victor and consoling the vanquished. They do it in simple ways: a high-five, a helmet butt, a pat on the bottom. I think they know instinctively what psychologists have been telling us for years. Recognition is a great motivator.

That is very different from those who say that too much praise will turn the recipient into an egomaniac. That's unlikely. Conceit is generally the fallout from too little praise, not too much. Narcissism is a defense mechanism, a way of compensating for the absence of recognition.

I've got it. Let's start a campaign to follow the lead of our professional athletes. The next time the boss makes a topnotch presentation to the board of directors, why not deliver a quick swat to the caboose. "Nice job, boss."

Success is worth a high-ten (or low-five) in any league.

THREE HUNDRED PEOPLE jammed the smoke-filled ballroom. A country-western band banged out "Your Cheatin' Heart." It was Friday night in a logging town, and the cowboys were restless.

A buckaroo with a string tie and a hefty paunch cascading over what must have been a rodeo belt buckle actually shouted, "YAAA-HOO!" It was clear the yelp was not meant to be satirical; there's no mistaking an authentic yahoo.

It was my first professional job — 50 bucks, an absolute fortune. All I had to do was play my guitar and sing for 30 minutes. It didn't seem that tough.

A short man with bushy eyebrows made my introduction. A few people applauded out of sheer boredom. I strapped on my guitar and walked to the microphone at the center of the dance floor. A pearl of sweat dropped from the end of my nose.

Someone belched.

I strummed a minor chord and sang the opening line from the "Love Theme from Romeo and Juliet"; it was one of the few songs I knew by heart.

> *A time for us*
> *Someday there'll be . . .*

Suddenly, someone in the back of the room shouted, "Take up tennis." I'm not making this up; I can still hear him. His voice was so loud I could smell the beer on his breath.

I knew I was losing them, but I didn't know what to do. I tried to bleach them out by looking directly into the stage spotlight; it didn't help. I stood there unprotected, the cold sweat trickling down my chest and irrigating all the creases.

I quickly finished and scrambled off to a small room behind the bandstand, my spirit snuffed out like a crumpled cigarette butt. Two people clapped, or maybe it was just the sound of a swat on someone's rump—I'm not sure.

I was packing up my guitar when suddenly the house erupted with laughter and applause. I poked my head out to see what had happened. The band was playing "The Stripper." A man in his late forties was dressed up like a woman and doing a strip tease. He got down to a flowered girdle and plastic falsies with tassels. He spun those tassels like two airplane props. And the crowd went crazy. They stomped and howled and cat-whistled. When it was over, he got a standing ovation.

That experience taught me a hard lesson. If you expect to make contact, it's imperative to gain rapport. By that I mean you have to speak the native language. I did not speak cowboyese, and that is why I lost my audience.

So if you're ever asked to sing at a cowboy honky-tonk, put a whine in your voice and a twang in your guitar; "*O Sole Mio*" ain't gonna cut it.

ONE YEAR MY WIFE AND I lived in a third-story apartment in Grenoble, France. We were studying French at the University. That summer I decided to enroll in a four-week actor's camp to be conducted in a small town about 200 miles away. My wife elected to stay in Grenoble and continue her studies.

As soon as I arrived at the camp, I knew I was in for a cultural awakening. The tipoff was the young French girl sunbathing in the nude at the courtyard pool. When I walked by, she smiled and said, "Bonjour." I wanted to say something cavalier like "Spiffy suit," but my French was still sketchy, so I just said "hello." I think my voice squeaked.

Later that first week, several of the young actors decided to go swimming at a nearby stream. I was invited. When we got there everyone stripped. There I sat in the sand — the only one wearing trunks—trying to decide where to look. Again, I pretended to be nonchalant, but what do you say to a naked French lady at a picnic? "Oops, you dropped a little potato salad on your— err—*Arc de Triomphe.*"

It was all new to me. Like the woman who slept one night with my roommate and the next night with her visiting husband—and back again.

By the end of camp, I was ready to go home. In fact, I left one day early around midnight. On the long trip back I kept thinking about all I had seen and how I longed to be home.

It was about 3:30 in the morning when I drove in. I got out of the car and looked up at our apartment. "Oh, my God, no." The lights in the bedroom were still on. In an instant, a full-length movie played in my head. I saw myself chasing up the apartment stairs, crashing through the front door, and finding my wife in the throws of uncontrollable, continental passions. I could see him now: long, black hair slicked back, reeking of cheap Parisian cologne. "Aarg, I'll massacre the guy!"

I took the elevator to the third floor. I unlocked the front door. I walked directly to the

bedroom. The door was shut. I turned the knob
and pushed in. It was jammed; there was a chair
braced against the door from the inside. (Ha! As
if that could stop me!) I called out to my wife,
wondering if a Frenchman could survive a leap from
a third-floor window.

My wife came to the door. Sleep was in her
eyes. She smiled sweetly and put her arms around
my neck. "I'm so glad you're home," she said. "I
was afraid to be alone tonight."

"I knew that," I lied. What else could I say?

It is a wonderful faculty, this thing we call
imagination, yet deceptively dangerous. For a light
turned on in the middle of the night may be
nothing more than a deflector of shadows or a
beacon for the homeward bound.

IN THE SUMMER OF 1972, my wife and I traced the Spanish Mediterranean coastline in a two-hundred-dollar Volkswagen bug. It was our first time in Spain, and I was thrilled. The sky was a baby blue, freshly squeezed out of the tube. The air felt like hot chocolate going down. And then there was the water. I waded chest-high into the Mediterranean and could still see the little black hairs sprouting from my big toes; it was that clear.

"Can you believe it?" I chirped to my wife. "We're actually in Spain—land of Don Quixote and flamenco dancers and Spanish pilaf!"

"Uh huh."

"And Pablo Picasso and gallant *caballeros* and the running of the bulls, and . . ." I stopped mid-sentence. Wait a minute; what did she mean "uh huh"? What kind of a response was that? "Uh

huh" was hardly the appropriate response for this
occasion. Where were the passion and fire and
"*oles*"?

"Okay, what's the matter?" I droned.

"Nothing's the matter."

"I know something's the matter; I can tell.
Now, tell me; what's the matter?"

My voice was starting to quiver. Something
was not right here. I was practically trembling
with excitement, and all my wife could manage was
an enthusiastic yawn. What was wrong? I looked
at her like she was something just squashed on the
highway.

"Aren't you excited?" I whined.

"Yes, I am—quite," she said with, what
seemed to me, the dignity and formality you might
use to address the Queen of England.

"Yes, I am—quite," I mocked. "No one
speaks like that. Cary Grant doesn't even speak
like that."

"I'm sorry," she said softly.

"What are you sorry about? Did I say you had
anything to be sorry about?" I was beginning to
talk crazy now. I was forcing an argument because
my wife was not behaving as I thought she should.

She was not excited. We were in Spain—land of romance and intrigue—and she, I had decided, was responding like a Saturday morning visit to the laundromat. What was wrong?

That was in 1972. I have learned a lot since then. I now realize that my wife *was* excited. In fact, on an expressiveness scale of one to ten, she was clearly into two digits, brimming with emotion. But when it comes to expressiveness, her ten is equal to my three.

There is nothing to fault and no one to blame; we are simply calibrated differently. Through the years I have come to understand that. I know now that a slight raise in pitch or volume from my wife —unrecognized by the untrained observer—is evidence of tremendous passion.

Today, when my wife says in her calm and collected voice "I believe I'm quite excited," I break out the champagne and the party hats.

WHEN I WAS A CHILD, I used to love the feeling of waking up from a nap. My eyes half opened, I would shuffle into the living room and find my mother sitting in the big, brown Lazyboy rocker.

"Hello, Sunshine; did you have a good nap?" she would ask.

I never said anything; I was always too sleepy. I simply fell into her lap as if I had just been shot. When I was older, I draped over her like a blanket, all limbs suddenly boneless. My mother enfolded me in her arms, smoothing the cowlick that sprouted from my crown like a carrot stalk.

During those moments, the sense of tranquility was absolute. It was a feeling of love, security, reassurance. I felt totally at peace with myself and the world—vulnerable, yet fully protected.

I am convinced that we require those moments

of reassurance—what I call a sanctuary of love
and protection—our entire lives; it is a longing
we simply do not outgrow.

The question is, how do we satisfy that need as
adults? True, mothers still remain a good source of
sustenance. My mom occasionally reminds me of
that fact.

"Give your mom a hug," she instructs me. "I'm
still your mother, Mister Smarty Britches." (There is
something leveling about a 44-year-old man being
called "Mister Smarty Britches.")

But moms are not always around. Even if they
were, I'm not sure that they would want to accept
the full-time position again. Mothers are nurturing,
but they also take great satisfaction in seeing their
dumpling darlings independent and out on their own.
So where do you go to be refueled?

For me, my refuge is my home. I know my
wife will be there, and I will get my hug, and she
will get hers. But sometimes she is not there. I
hit the garage door opener; the panel is two feet
off the ground, and I can see her car is gone. I
always feel a little sadness when that happens. Not
because I think it's her purpose in life to greet me
at the door—she has her career too—but

because my hug gets delayed, and when it comes to hugs, I believe in instant gratification.

When my wife is home and we embrace, my whole being is grateful: "Oh, thank you, thank you, great hug-giver; I needed that." Her warmth radiates through me like a convection oven. Somehow that squeeze reassures me that I'm okay. I know that, but still it's nice to get confirmation.

Later in the evening, after we've talked about the events of the day, I turn on the stereo, stretch out on the couch, and let the music wash over me like a tropical wave. That is sustenance too. I am home: loved, safe, and protected.

I shared these ideas with a friend of mine who is single. "Do you have a need for a sanctuary?" I asked.

"Of course," she said. "I think having that special person is ideal; I would like that some day, but I am not going to fall apart because I don't have it now. For the time being, I satisfy my need in other ways."

"How's that?" I asked.

"It helps to have my dog to come home to," she said. "He's funny; he knocks himself out to greet me."

"Is that all?" I secretly hoped not. I've seen her dog; to me, he looks like a shaggy mouse with a vocal disorder.

"There are my friends," she continued. "I work very hard at maintaining those relationships. Sometimes I'll have a couple over for some popcorn and a movie. Or maybe I'll just call and find out how they're doing."

My friend is taking care of business. She knows, perhaps instinctively, that she must routinely attend to her need for belonging. At the same time, she is mature enough to enjoy the quiet solitude of her own company.

Single or married, we need those nurturing moments — a time to wake up in the lap of love and security.

I've never thought about it until just now, but I can't remember my mother ever breaking the hug first; I was always the first to pull away, scrambling off to some childhood adventure. Was she making certain that I was fully charged? Or, could it be that I was *her* sanctuary too?

ONCE A YEAR I like to bang out my personal goals for the next twelve months. It is my way of willfully and deliberately selecting the road I will travel.

One year I decided to work harder at making friends. I wrote down the names of five people I admired. I wanted to be closer to them, to have a connection, to be able to say, "You are my friend, and I feel proud." I began to think of those five people as my "Golden Friends."

But how do you create that kind of relationship? Friendship is not something you can mandate. "Hey, you, be my friend or I'll break your legs." No, that doesn't work. So I simply decide to be myself, speaking directly and honestly.

One by one I approached the "Golden Five." I explained to them what I had in mind.

"I am looking for five good friends," I said

bluntly. "People I can talk to openly, free of criticism or pretense. I'm looking for a kindred spirit, a person who would immediately understand the meaning of a knowing wink or gentle poke to the ribs. Are you willing?"

It was a pretty brazen thing to ask when I think about it. But do you know what I discovered? All five were a little stunned and considerably tickled by my openness. But mostly, they were flattered that I should ask. And I was flattered that they were flattered.

Each of them said, "Yes, I would be delighted to be your Golden Friend."

That was several years ago now. Some of them I see only rarely. But when we do meet, there is a connection. Recently, I ran into Mary Lou, one of the "Golden Five," at a seminar. We spotted each other, smiled, and embraced.

"Hey, Allen," an observer teased, "what's the deal? I didn't get a hug."

"Ah, yes," Mary Lou quipped, "but are you one of the Golden Friends?"

That was a nice moment. (Not to mention the pleasure of a second hug from the dissenting bystander.)

Here's the point. Making friends takes some risk. The "Golden Five" could have told me to take a hike, although I think that would have been unlikely; people generally respond favorably to an invitation for friendship. Still, you do have to be willing to be somewhat vulnerable.

Susan is a good example. When I first met her, I was taken by her natural charm. She was poised and articulate. But she was also careful; there was a thin veil of protection that separated the two of us. I was not troubled by it; I just noted its presence. In time, when she felt more comfortable with me, she looked me in the eyes and told me her story.

When she did that, I was both thrilled and honored. Susan had allowed herself to become accessible — to say "This is who I am; I hope you like me." It is my responsibility to protect that trust. If I do not, the relationship will fail. It is that simple and that important. There is no greater responsibility and no greater joy.

SCOTT IS FIFTEEN YEARS OLD. He is athletic, congenial, and good looking. He's the sort of young man that girls giggle over in the school hallways. He has style and charisma. And now, at fifteen, he has cancer.

I am not worried about Scott; I am concerned, but not worried. His family and extended family are a powerhouse; they are loving—totally committed to each other. As for Scott, he is strong and vital; he will beat it. In fact, I expect that the experience will kindle a maturity far beyond his years.

So, this is not a sob story; Scott wouldn't buy that, anyway. This is a story about friendship.

After Scott was diagnosed with cancer, he underwent chemotherapy. As a result, he began losing his hair. It came out in tufts, first from the sides and then all over; it looked pretty scraggly.

How does a kid deal with that?

His sister, home from college, had an idea. She got out a safety razor and the family shears and went to work. She shaved the sides smooth, leaving a short crop of stubble on the crown of his head. It looked a little like a *severe* Marine haircut.

That's the way he went to school, glossy on the sides, butch on the top.

Then it happened. Several of Scott's friends decided they wanted the same coiffure. They trooped over to Scott's house after school and asked his sister to render the honors.

At first, Scott's mother protested. "Your school pictures will be taken tomorrow," she argued.

But the boys would have nothing to do with that. "If we can't support Scott today," they said, "we are not worthy of his friendship. Get out the shears."

One by one the boys sat down on a straight-back chair in the middle of the kitchen floor, a dish towel draped around their necks. The shears clicked on and the clumps of hair dropped silently to the floor.

Scott's father smiled. "These boys are going

though the fire together," he thought, "and they will never again be the same."

"Sis," he said to his daughter after the last boy stood up from the kitchen chair, "I'm next."

A year has passed since I wrote that story. Scott is now a sophomore in high school. At his last visit to the doctor, he was given a clean bill of health. The cancer is gone. And Scott is the sixth man on the varsity, regional champion basketball team. Scott, you are a winner!

HENRY WAS A BAD BOY. He was not criminal, just mean. He was the kind of kid who always took cuts in the lunch line at school. He made obscene grumblings in the back of his throat when the teacher sat down—BRruuUMP—and then blamed it on the fat kid with glasses who was too nervous to defend himself. He scratched dirty words on the bathroom walls with his Schlitz Malt Liquor pocket knife. ("You want to have a good time? Call Louise." Louise was the school librarian and about as sensual as a textbook on quantum physics.)

Nobody liked Henry. He was crude, impolite, and selfish. By the time he graduated from high school—that in itself the eighth wonder of the world—he was voted "Most Likely to Mug a Nun."

Then a curious thing happened. One summer

day Henry was sitting on a park bench, pelting pigeons with chunks of gravel, when a young lady sat down beside him. Her name was Cindy. She was friendly and very pretty—in the way all women are pretty when they value themselves.

"Good morning," Cindy said cheerfully.

The greeting startled Henry. Her voice was so pleasant, he guessed she must be speaking to someone else. But, with the exception of the dazed pigeons, they were alone.

"Uh, hi," he finally stammered.

"You must not like pigeons very much," Cindy said.

"Ah, they're okay, I guess, if you like that sort of thing."

"What *do* you like?" Cindy asked softly.

Henry looked suspiciously at this friendly stranger. Her voice was free of the surliness he was accustomed to when people spoke to him. She seemed truly interested in his opinion.

"I don't know," Henry finally mumbled. "What's there to like?"

"You mean, you feel like there's nothing that can make you smile?"

With that Henry *did* smile. It was not

something he did very often; you could almost hear his cheeks crackle like cellophane. "You'll probably think this is dumb," Henry said, "but I've always liked bugs, especially black beetle bugs."

"I don't think that's dumb," Cindy said. "Tell me about it."

So, Henry talked about bugs. And Cindy listened. She did not criticize; she did not make judgments. She simply tried to understand Henry's world as he experienced it. She entered his perceptual domain and made herself at home, experiencing for herself his thoughts and feelings. She activated that human quality that almost instantly makes the confused less troubled: empathy.

The deeper she entered Henry's world, the more real he became. He was no longer mean and vindictive. Rather, he was relaxed and calm and more sure of himself.

That is the magic of empathy. It clearly moves people toward more positive attitudes and behavior. It helps them gain new insight into their person-hood—rich discoveries that are eventually blended into their self-concept. They feel under-stood, less alienated from the rest of the world.

Mostly, though, they feel recognized as a person of worth. And when that happens, they no longer have to compensate by devaluing themselves or ridiculing others. There's no need; people of worth have a new appreciation for all humanity.

Oh, you may be wondering about Henry and Cindy. They are quite happy, thank you. Henry says that he has the best of two worlds: an understanding wife and the finest collection of black beetles in North America. Who could ask for anything more?

CHAPTER ONE: SEX

And then their eyes met. Jack was quite certain that he had never seen a woman quite so lovely. Her name was Farah. The grace of her ankles, the elegance of her long, alabaster neck, the ever-so-slight overbite, leaving her soft, full lips perpetually pursed—it was all too, too intoxicating. Jack wanted to kiss those lips. No, that's not right; he wanted to devour them. He was only sixteen, and his hormones were not saving up for retirement.

CHAPTER TWO: AFFECTION

Jack is much older now. There are other women in his life, including Clara, who works in the same office. They have known each other for seven years. Although there isn't much that Jack and Clara don't know about one another, they are not lovers. They are just good friends; you can tell that in the way they treat each other. They share a smile, a funny story about home, a pat on the arm. There is a lot of comfort there, a lot of affection.

CHAPTER THREE: LOVE

Jack is not without love. He met Sarah at his first job out of college. Within six months they were married; that was twenty years ago. Over the years they have had their share of struggles and disappointments—unemployment, escalating bills, quarrelsome in-laws—but through it all they always maintained a sense of commitment to each other. Yes, there was sex; and, yes, there was affection; but at the heart, there was love.

I chose to introduce Jack and his three women to make a point. Sex, affection, and love are not synonymous. I know it seems obvious, but many get the words jumbled in their heads. Let's see if we can untangle their meaning.

Confusion about sex. When Jack met Farah, he thought he was in love. His reasoning was simple. If kissing her felt that good, it *must* be love. Jack is not alone; many people confuse runaway passion with true love. The fact is, sex and love serve separate needs. Sex serves the primitive and instinctual sex-need. It is internally regulated in the same way we control for hunger and thirst. Although the drive is enormously powerful, any single urge can be satisfied in a matter of minutes. Love, on the other hand, serves a higher more social love-need. It is about how we connect with the world. The desire is on-going.

Those who attempt to satisfy their love-need with casual sex are destined to feel empty and used. The morning after, when the passion has subsided, they wonder, "What was that all about?"

Fooled again, and no wonder. The mass media have programmed us to believe that sex buys permanent love. How can you look at those smiling, vibrant faces and not believe that lasting happiness is just a pair of blue jeans away?

Confusion about affection. Jack and his co-worker, Clara, remain affectionate without being sexual. There is no confusion about their intentions. They simply take time to recognize each other as people — quite a departure from treating the other as an object: a typewriter or a staple machine.

In the realm of marriage, some spouses offer affection only as an overture to sex. It doesn't take a partner long to recognize and resent the routine. The gesture is soon viewed as cheap and manipulative. In time sex may be withheld or granted dispassionately out of some sense of obligation.

Confusion about love. Jack and his wife Sarah know what makes love last: work. They are affectionate and their sex is good, but at the core they are busy keeping their love fresh. How do they do that?

They practice perceiving one another positively. They see the good in each other; they are sensitive to the fine qualities that often go unnoticed by outsiders. When they can't be positive, when the actions of the other are too hard to swallow, they practice perceiving the event with indifference. Why? Because it is abundantly less damaging to the relationship than negative criticism. A marriage would never abide constant indifference, but if used prudently, it can be healthy.

Jack and Sarah are also committed to each other. That commitment was sealed in their decision to marry. They have said, "Yes, we are willing to take the risk. We are committed to making our marriage work. We will not run at the first hint of a crisis; we will see it through — together."

Sex, affection, and love. If Jack can manage to keep the differences straight, he will realize a lot more happiness and a lot less heartache. If he cannot, the final chapter in the book of love could turn into a horror story.

CHAPTER FOUR: THE ENCOUNTER

Unbeknown to Jack, Farah, Clara, and Sarah arrived at the same dinner party. Jack had no choice but to make the introductions. "Farah, Clara. Clara, Farah. Sarah, Clara. Clara, Sarah. Sarah, Farah. Farah, Sarah. Clara I like. Farah I want. Sarah I like, want, and need. Or was it Clara that I want and Sarah that I like and Farah that I need. Or maybe it was . . ."

And with that Jack O'Hara turned and slipped into the night and was never seen or heard of again—except once . . . on the highway to Santa Clara. But that's another story.

"LET'S GO FOR IT," I said.

"Why not? It's probably the only way she's gonna kiss me; she's so dang sweet. It just seems like a dirty trick."

"Hey, will you knock it off?" I squawked. "It'll be fun."

"Yeah, I guess so."

He didn't sound convinced. Hank was my best friend in high school. He had been dating Kathy for over a month. It took him three weeks to work up to holding her hand. At that rate he might land a peck on her cheek by the turn of the century. So, I devised this delicious scheme.

"Okay, it's settled," I said. "We pretend both of us have been drafted into the army. And we're taking the train to boot camp, right? You know she's gotta kiss you at the train station."

"It works in the movies," Hank admitted

sheepishly. "I just hope we don't hurt . . ."

I cut him off; I didn't want to hear another wimpy argument. I've always had a passion for the dramatic, and this idea was pure Hollywood.

The plan was foolproof: a tearful goodbye, the fateful kiss, and some fancy footwork to get on and off the train without leaving the station. Afterwards, Hank and I would double back to Kathy's house and sock her with a song and dance routine when she opened the front door. "Hey, we're back, we're back. It was only a joke. We must be the funniest guys on earth."

I have wised up a little since then. I have learned that it is cruel to toy with someone's emotions. It is equivalent to criminal fraud: intentional deception to gain control of another's property. In this case, the property was Kathy's emotions. Look around; emotional fraud is not far away. Here are a few examples that come to mind.

The Flirt. In the battle for social or psychological power, some women and men will use their sex appeal to arouse their conquest. When the victim responds to the overtures, the flirt screams "Rape!" That is the flirt's payoff. Other "punch lines" include: "What kind of woman do you think

I am?" or "You are a horny devil, aren't you?" or
"All of you are the same—one-track mind." The
victim is left feeling confused and somehow
inexplicably ashamed.

The Comic. Once I visited a friend who told
me that he had a new gun he wanted to show me.

"I'll be right back," he said, disappearing into
his bedroom.

A moment later, there was a gun blast, and he
staggered into the room and collapsed on the living
room floor. Before I could reach him, he leapt to
his feet and struck a clownish pose.

"It's just a starter's pistol," he grinned.

Why wasn't I laughing?

The Coach. In both business and athletics,
there are those who adopt the role of an angry
coach, bellowing insults at their players with the
intention of inflaming their passion to win. Such
tactics are ineffectual for a number of reasons.
People of any age do not respond positively to
personal attack. Oh, they may wear a mask of
compliance, but underneath they will create ways of
sabotaging the coach's goals.

Equally important, players perform best when
they are relaxed. The brain makes quick, targeted

decisions; the body responds smoothly, instinctively, to the moves and countermoves of the opponent. When assaulted by a furious coach, that state of efficiency is replaced by mental and physical tension and, ultimately, a clumsy performance.

The Parent. Some adults choose to toy with the emotions of their children. A popular tactic is to say "Just wait until your father comes home, young man; you're going to get it." The kid doesn't know what "it" is; he just knows he should be worried. When the father does come home, he may choose to ignore the crime. For the mother that is almost inconsequential; she's already gained what she wanted. The child has been held emotional hostage for the entire day.

These are just a few of the ways that people toy with the emotions of others. The list is far from complete. The point is that the ploy is cheap and dehumanizing. In the long run it results in resentment and damaged relationships. I should know.

My scheme for Hank and Kathy did work. Kathy drove us to the train station. We stood around the terminal for a few minutes and looked at each other's shoes. Finally, Hank put his arms around Kathy and kissed her full on the mouth. Then we talked her into leaving first because "saying goodbye was too painful to bear."

I will never forget the look on Kathy's face when we leveled with her. It was not exactly the look of contempt; it was more like grief, as though she had just lost a dear friend. And in a way she had. Hank never did get a second kiss.

I WAS SITTING in the Las Vegas airport, reading a discarded, day-old *Los Angeles Times* when I heard my name called over the intercom.

"Mister Allen Johnson, please return to the checkout counter."

Oh-oh, what was wrong? Were my tickets out of order? Were they overbooked? Was there an emergency at home?

"We are changing your seating assignment, Mr. Johnson," the attendant said smiling. "We need a little more room in coach."

I looked at my new boarding pass. The number was 3B. I had never seen a number that low before. Three-B? Hey, that was first class! That's cool, I said to myself; I can handle that. Instantly, I was transformed into the Dalai Lama of business tycoons. I puffed out my chest, flared my nostrils, and draped my topcoat over my shoulders —

continental style, both arms outside the sleeves.

I was the last to board—after all the riffraff. Everything about me said, "Yes, I am wealthy, I am successful, I am every woman's wildest desire." (Hey, why not? It's my fantasy. I can think whatever I want.)

A moment later I was seated in an overstuffed, leather lounge chair. There was enough room for two of me. I crossed my legs with a flair and then gaged the depth of the seat cushion with a few surreptitious vertical plunges of my buttocks. "Deep."

"May I serve you a drink?" asked the perky flight attendant. She seemed more gracious, more fawning than any hostess I had ever encountered in coach. I was more accustomed to "Hey, you. That's right, you, the one trying to sleep. Catch your nuts."

I almost asked for a glass of "the bubbly," and then remembered that I didn't drink alcohol. So I said, "Yes, a ginger ale if you will," and then in a stroke of inspiration added, "with a twist." Classic!

As soon as we were in flight, the perky attendant was at my elbow again. "Sir, will we be dining this evening?"

I giggled in spite of myself. I had never *dined*
on an airplane in my entire life. I have nibbled,
munched, even scarfed, but never dined.

"Indeed," I said, regaining my composure.

A moment later the flight attendant was
standing over me with a three-foot square of linen.
For a moment I thought that she was going to tuck
it in under my chin for me. I put my book down
and smiled up at her.

"Let me assist you," she said. She popped the
cover of my armrest, exhumed the double-fold table,
and delicately flipped the small linen tablecloth into
place.

My silverware — that's right, silverware —
was also wrapped in linen. There was a knife, a
fork, a spoon, and a cute little set of salt and
pepper shakers. Yes, I would be truly dining.

That was on the first leg of my trip back
home. On the second leg I was in coach again,
back in the galley with my friends, Riff and Raff.
I sat with my knees squeezed together like a
modest debutante in a high-water skirt, protecting
the world from indiscretion. I looked longingly
through the slit in the curtain that separates the
world of first class from the world of coach. How

agonizing to have once known the pleasures of aristocracy and then to huddle unadorned with the proletariat, fallen from grace.

I think everyone should experience flying first class. I plan, as a matter of routine, to volunteer my services anytime coach looks a little cramped for space. After all, I am worthy of primo service; I deserve to be pampered now and then.

Ah, but then there is the question of money; how often can I afford to fly in luxury? Not often. But I can afford to treat myself with first-class respect, attending to my personal needs with the same standards of service embraced by the best of first-class flight attendants.

I've decided. I plan to be gracious to me: speak well of myself and bathe in luxury from time to time. Heck, I'm worth it. I'm a first-class passenger, despite seating assignment 38B, one row this side of luggage.

I WANTED TO SEE FOR MYSELF what it was like. I had read about Pamplona, Spain, in books by Ernest Hemingway. I had seen photographs of men with white shirts and red bandannas charging slam-bam down a narrow street, a raging bull in wild pursuit, plunging and tromping the most clumsy of runners.

And, yes, there was that, but much, much more.

The day we arrived, my wife and I set up camp alongside the Arga River just outside Pamplona. After dinner—a few slices of salami and cheese on French bread—we drove into town.

It was dark now. The air was warm and a little sultry; it was beginning to drizzle. The streets were jammed with tourists, all of them, like us, wandering aimlessly, taking in the scent and sounds of Pamplona. In the distance we could hear the night thunder tumbling on the hillside.

Soon the drizzle became a light shower and
then a driving rain. People darted into darkened
doorways and nuzzled there, waiting for the rain to
let up, giggling and whispering in Spanish or French
or German. No one went home.

My wife and I kept walking. We were at the
town square now. There was a small park with
grand old trees that formed a protective canopy
over the travelers who carpeted the grounds below.
Some 500 people crammed into the modest park; a
few huddled under small makeshift tents; most
sprawled side-by-side in blankets and sleeping bags.
I've never seen anything like it; it was as though
the mayor called a slumber party and the whole
town showed up.

Just then the sky erupted. The lightning came
crashing down, illuminating the town square. (Man
alive! There must have been a *thousand* people
under the trees.) And then the thunder. BOOM!
And again BOOM! And, yet, again BOOOOMMM!
It was incredible. The Almighty was crashing and
cracking and turning on every light in the house.
My God! It made you hold your breath.

And the people; I will never forget the people.
They applauded! With every rip of lightning, every

blast of thunder, they rose up in a single voice and cheered! And the louder the thunder rolled, the louder they bellowed. The bull was raging, and the crowd loved it. *"Toro! Toro! Toro!"*

I turned to my wife, overcome with joy. I held her in my arms, drenched in the pouring rain. I could say nothing.

That is a moment I remember when the lonely speak of dying, and the angry strike out, and the whiners and the moaners insist that people are no damn good. That is the moment I cling to, one summer night, when all of us were linked by a common love of peace and fellowship and the wonders of the universe, ready to join in, to throw our heads back and shout at the top of our voices, *"Toro! Toro! Toro!"*

AN INTERESTING THING HAPPENED at the company Christmas party this year. I danced with a half dozen lovely ladies, all decked out in their holiday gowns. That's not particularly noteworthy; I've danced with women in holiday gowns before. It might have been interesting if *I* had been decked out in a holiday gown, but that was not the case and, moreover, digresses from the point.

What was striking to me was the realization that each of my partners had one favorite dance step that carried her through the entire night. One step. One of my companions held out both hands, like a kid waiting to be spanked with a teacher's ruler, and then made little hand-circles, first clockwise and then counter clockwise. Initially, I thought, "Gee, that's kinda cute," but by the end of "Louie, Louie," I was considerably bored with the Eddie Cantor gesture.

So I danced with another partner.

"Ah ha," I said to myself, "I can see by your demeanor that you have rhythm."

And she did. Her right shoulder dipped to the off-beat and then rolled back on the on-beat. At the same time, her left knee buckled in and then out again. It looked real spiffy. But 16 measures into the song, 32 measures into the song, I was wondering when I might see another step: maybe a dip with the *left* shoulder and a buckle with the *right* knee — that would be a novelty. But no, 128 measures of dip right, buckle left.

I began to develop a theory. I hypothesized that sometime in junior high school each of my daring partners discovered a step that worked, a step that was conventional and efficient — but primarily a step that did not attract attention. When that movement was conceived, they latched on to it with a vengeance.

At that moment, each of these self-conscious teenagers experienced DANCE BRAIN DAMAGE. The circuits in their heads that control dance creativity blew up, and now that portion of cerebral hardware is a glob of mangled wire-endings and burnt PVC. With that, all dance learning stopped.

You could hear the soft, melancholic refrain of taps playing in the distance: *Ta-ta-taaa. Ta-ta-taaa.*

What if my theory is correct? Moreover, what if the same thing happens in all sectors of our lives?

Maybe we have eating brain damage: "I'm sorry. I only know how to eat pudding. My brain blew up before I was introduced to vegetables."

Or people brain damage: "I can't speak to you; I only talk to people who resemble my mother — brain damage, you know."

Is it possible we grab on to one thing that works and stick with it forever and ever, until death takes us home and we do the same thing in heaven?

How boring.

It is time to connect the wires, to clean out the caked PVC, to accept a new opportunity for growth. Sure, making little circles left and right works, but so do jabs and undulations and twirls and hip thrusts and, Willy Begonia, THE POSSIBILITIES ARE MIND-BOGGLING!

It is time to break out. It is time to ask ourselves some industrial-strength questions. If we did not have brain damage, how would our lives be different? How would our self-images be altered? What new career paths would we take? How would our relationships change? What new challenges would we accept?

Just once, I would like to have seen one courageous, brain-healthy dancer doing the alligator: flip-flopping on all fours, flamboozling the whole crowd.

Sure, it's risky.

And, yeah, it's different.

But it sure ain't boring.

ONE RECESS, during my short career as an elementary school music teacher, an eight-year-old girl took my hand, tilted her head back, and looked at the bottom side of my face. It was a new perspective for her. Suddenly, she announced in amazement, "Gee, you have little black hairs coming out of your nose."

Her observation made me laugh so loudly I think I startled her. "How wonderful," I thought, "to speak with such candor—innocent of all that is *proper* and *fitting*."

I love that quality in children; we could take a lesson from them. In fact, there is much that we could learn from our diminutive mentors. They are, after all, the most *natural* beings on earth.

While thinking this through, I have discovered something about myself. The people who I am most drawn to, the ones who I want to be around, are not afraid to be childlike. They are the ones who laugh, wink, joke, fantasize, play, explore, wonder, and use funny voices when they tell stories. In a phrase, they enjoy the moment.

If you had a choice — and you do — would you rather be childlike or grown-up? Before you answer, consider the differences.

The childlike are spontaneous, curious, and adventuresome; the grown-up are orderly, apathetic, and resigned to long stretches of boredom.

The childlike are genuine, straightforward, and accepting of others; the grown-up are guarded, secretive, and judgmental.

The childlike are trusting, silly, and refreshingly innovative; the grown-up are fearful, solemn, and victims of convention.

Being childlike has nothing to do with chronology. I know responsible adults of *every* age who are delightfully childlike. Conversely, I've met some twelve-year-olds who are sadly and thoroughly grown-up — strutting around self-consciously in stiff, pubescent bodies.

It's amazing how quickly a free-spirited child can be transformed into an uptight elder. It is no wonder when you consider how we scold our

youngsters for being childlike. "When are you going
to grow up?" "Don't be so childish." "Why don't
you act your age?" And these messages begin about
the time the infant learns to walk! It doesn't take
a genius to figure out how children will respond.
"I hate it when they holler; I better start acting
grown-up."

Regrettably, children learn very quickly to
abandon their natural instinct for fun and
spontaneity. They concentrate on being more like
their parents—rigid, judgmental, serious, and
humorless. Soon, they are condemning their
younger bothers and sisters for not being more
"mature." The cycle is never ending.

When I was eight years old, I lived in a trailer
court. There was a common washroom with three
showers and a couple of sinks. Every Saturday
night my brother and I would march over to take
our weekly bath—right, whether we needed it or
not. I will never forget those scrubbings. We took
something disgusting—getting clean, yuck!—
and turned it into a carnival. After we had
thoroughly soaped and rinsed, we cranked all three
showers to full hot. In minutes the washroom was

steaming, a soggy carton of wet, hot fog.

Then we did it. We went keister-sailing across the room on our gleaming, pink bottoms, hooting and hollering and crashing into porcelain. It's amazing how slick concrete gets with a thin film of steam.

I am smiling now as I write about that adventure. I even feel the old excitement gurgling in my stomach. I don't want to give that up. I want to slide on my labonza again and this time go for the world record.

"That's childish," you say?

Yes, it is. And thank you for noticing.

IT WAS SATURDAY MORNING. My wife and I were sitting in the living room, involved with our own projects. I was engrossed in a book that I had wanted to read for some time. It was absolutely quite. Suddenly, my wife started humming softly.

"HummmMMmmmmmmmm."

"Shh," I whispered, not looking up from my book.

A pause, and then about three clicks louder, "HUMMMMMmmHUMMMM."

I squelched my urge to smile. "Honey," I said in a voice usually reserved for small children and people with left and right sock drawers, "this is our quiet time. It's time to be quiet now. You know, quiet, as in no noise?"

Another pause. I returned to my book and started the same paragraph for the third time. I

was halfway into the first sentence when my wife
opened up with a UCLA Marching Band rendition of
"Stars and Stripes Forever."

"Ba-rum-bum-bum. Blah-dah-dah-dah-dah, blah-
dah-dah-dah-dah-KABOOM!"

She had the bass drum, the trombones, the
clarinets, and cymbals — 152 pieces, all pumping
out at triple forte.

After that it was impossible to keep a straight
face. I had no choice but to laugh out loud. And
that felt good. Laughter is, after all, a kind of
natural tranquilizer without the side effects.

That incident was a reminder to me of the
importance of playfulness in our lives. In one ten-
second musical interlude, my wife put things into
perfect perspective: "Hey, life does not have to be
all that serious."

I've noticed that including a little levity in the
day's activities diminishes the storehouse of stress
felt at the end of the day. So, here are a few
playful ideas for your consideration.

The next time you call someone and get a
recording, wait for the beep and then pretend that
their machine has broken down. Imitate a 78 rpm
record played on 33.

"Hello, this is Aaaallleeeen Urrrhgummmn. Congratulations! You've just won ten thousand dollars! But you must call me IMMEDIATELY at aargherschplout."

Or how about this one? The next time you're at a tollbooth, pay the fifty cents for the person directly behind you. It's great. They race like crazy to catch up with you, absolutely certain that you are the dearest of friends. They pull up to the side of your car and wave wildly. Then at that instant, when they realize that you are a complete stranger, their expression transforms from frenzied jubilation to total bewilderment. That look alone is worth the 50 cents.

Or try this where you work. Ask the people in your group to bring a baby picture of themselves to the job. Mount the pictures on a bulletin board and enjoy the fun of guessing "who's who." Even the stuffiest is suddenly humanized when pictured in the buff on a bear rug.

All I'm saying is that life is worth living with a smile. After all, things could be worse. *You* could be married to a brass band.

IT NEVER FAILS. I'm playing basketball at
the city park, right? I'm having a good time
jostling with the guys under the backboard —
leaning in a little on the drives. Then, at the end
of the game, this big 250-pound lug with bib
overalls tries to dunk the ball. He can't do it, of
course, but he gets high enough to grab the rim
and hang there like a bloated Christmas bulb. And,
naturally, the rim drops about an inch.

The last time that happened, I spoke up.

"Hey!" I barked, "don't do that." If I had
stopped there, it would have been fine. I didn't. I
decided my demand required a descriptive title to
underscore the seriousness of the crime. "Hey!
don't do that, CLOWN!"

That was a mistake. The joker whipped his
head around, peeled back his lips, and made a lewd
remark about the legitimacy of my birth.

About that time someone suggested we play another game. I knew I would be guarding Clarabell; suddenly, "jostling with the guys" lost a large chunk of appeal. So I bowed out, making up some virile excuse, like having to mount a gun rack on my four-wheel-drive pickup truck.

That is one way to deal with conflict—to push back. But "pushing back" almost always escalates the dialogue and aggravates the situation. It becomes a name-calling contest; the person with the most colorful vocabulary or heaviest fist wins.

When I shared these thoughts with a friend recently, he quoted a line from a book by Chris Griscom: "Where there is no resistance, there is no harm." At first, the statement didn't make sense to me, but the more I thought about it, the more I liked it. Why, of course, there is safety in letting go. I can resist the 250-pound lug—and possibly have my teeth reshuffled in the transaction—or I can let go, stating my case as an adult if necessary, but avoiding hostility.

Griscom's statement is in line with an image of civility and tranquility that I've been carrying around in my head lately. I call it the "Silent Samurai."

The "Silent Samurai" is the person who is calm,
self-assured, at peace with himself and his sur-
roundings. He is mentally disciplined, physically
powerful, and spiritually centered. But he does not
need to boast or flex his muscles. He has nothing
to prove; he is fully aware of his virtues and
shortcomings and, at the same time, acceptant of
the condition of others.

The "Silent Samurai" is a mighty warrior; he
can move with the quickness of a cat. Still, he
seldom strikes. His inner peace tempers his
aggression and dissuades his opponents. When he
does act, it is more like a dance. He simply flows
with the thrust of his assailant, who tumbles to the
ground under his own force.

I would like to be like a "Silent Samurai." Just
think how liberating that would be. No longer
would I have to prove my toughness or cleverness
or superiority. No longer would I have to "beat up"
on people, like some stag asserting my position in
the herd.

Perhaps you're thinking, "Yeah, but sometimes
you have to stand up and fight. Otherwise, they'll
walk all over you."

I agree in part. I do believe you have to stand

up for what you value. But I do not believe in fighting.

Let's replay the incident at the park. I think my best strategy would have been to speak as an adult.

"You know, all of us use this court, and it's a lot more fun when the rim is level. I, for one, would appreciate it if you didn't hang on it."

That is a straight message; there is nothing disparaging about that statement. And most people will respond favorably. But what if he doesn't? What if he keeps at it?

At that point I need to remember that I am not responsible for his behavior; it is not my job to fix him. Force of any kind—even a threat to call the police—is unlikely to change his style.

I think my best choice is simply to walk away. To resist further would only result in harm. That does not make me a pacifist, for a battle is still raging, an inner battle to preserve my personal dignity. For me, that is the only struggle worth pursuing.

FOR TWO YEARS my wife and I lived in an
Algerian mountain village fifty miles south of the
Mediterranean Sea. The town was called Larbaa
Nath Irathen, which means "market day is on
Thursday." True to its name, every Thursday
morning the narrow streets and open shops teemed
with Berbers from the surrounding farms and
villages, bartering over woolens, figs, and long-
haired goats.

I was especially fond of the meat market.
There was never any question about what was fresh;
the head of the "animal of the day" was mounted on
a hook on the storefront wall like a big game
trophy. They looked like incarnate gargoyles,
tongues unfurled, all with the same pathetic
expression: "Holy cow, was it something I said?"

There were no women on the streets—only
men wrapped in their burnooses, squatting flat-

footed on the roadside, their elbows between their
legs. They looked like Moslem baseball catchers
waiting for the delivery.

My wife and I taught English at the public high
school. Every morning we walked through town to
go to school. Every afternoon we walked back,
stopping at Abdul's "full-service super marche" for
the day's groceries: a couple of artichokes, a few
oranges, and the ever-present couscous, a kind of
African farina without the lumps.

Each walk through town was a little like "Babes
on Parade"—my wife on center stage. Where she
walked, one thousand pairs of eyes followed. There
were times I swore I heard a Berber chant, "Sha-
boom, chic-chic-boom, chic-chic-boom."

Those were strange days. And we were
strangers in a strange land. The sounds, the smells,
the customs—they were all new. It was like
nothing either of us had ever known. It was
sometimes scary, sometimes frustrating, and even
occasionally infuriating.

But despite all that, we adjusted. In fact,
those two years were a time of terrific growth. We
learned how to entertain ourselves without the
questionable benefit of *The Dukes of Hazard* or

Bowling for Dollars. We read, wrote short stories,
painted, composed music, developed friendships, and
absorbed an intriguing and ancient culture.

In short, we adapted. It was no big deal —
we merely tapped the resources that we all share.
People exhibit incredible elasticity under crisis?
When a home is destroyed, they rebuild. When a
family is shaken, they pull together. When a
business fails, they take another tack — they
reset, they bounce back. That is the way people
are; we have a wonderful aptitude for survival.

Yes, there are those who buckle under in times
of change, but they are in the minority. They are
the unfortunate ones who have not yet learned that
they have what it takes: the intelligence and will
to make it work. They were not born with self-
doubt; they learned it along the way. They are the
children who were dismissed as losers, the wives
who were labeled stupid, the elderly who were
written off as feebleminded. That is not uncommon;
many of us have been told such rubbish. The
difference is they gradually grew to accept it.

We often hear that people are designed for
success. I believe it. The cruel and misguided
voices of the past and present that tell us

otherwise are to be pitied for their own insecurity. I will not listen to those unhappy voices. I resolve that when change comes, as it always does, that I will stand ready to assert, "Shoot, let me at it; I can handle it."

THIS IS A STORY ABOUT TWO MEN who
made a difference in my life: one as my opponent,
the other as my mentor. Although they never met,
each man possessed what the other lacked.

One summer between my sophomore and junior
year in college, I landed a job at the local paper
mill. I was thrilled. I don't remember what my
salary was, but it beat anything I could earn at
Gene and Jules Grocery Store.

My first day I rode out to the plant with a few
of the old timers. They talked about their weekend.

"Hell," one of them said, "I got so drunk Friday
night I puked all over Sally May."

The others laughed. I managed to work up a
half smile; I hoped it suggested that I was something of a hoochhound myself. In truth I had

always thought Dr. Pepper had a little too much
bite. I wondered what Sally May looked like. I
pictured a plump, bleached blond with stop-sign-red
lipstick and a proclivity for cleavage.

The morning of that first day I worked with a
group that bound and stacked broken-down card-
board boxes onto wooden pallets. The load was
hauled away by a fork lift and restacked on the
other side of the warehouse. It was not fun.
Almost immediately I envied the man who drove the
fork lift; criminy, it was the guy who barfed on
Sally May. I breathed a long languish sign. I
didn't think it was the kind of assignment they
gave to a kid who couldn't handle a Dr. Pepper.

After lunch there was a small miracle. The
foreman, a swarthy middle-aged biker with bad
teeth, tapped me on the shoulder.

"Johnson, follow me."

I was ecstatic.

"You see that press," he said. It looked like a
giant waffle iron with raised, one-inch-high letters
laid out in mirror image across the cast-iron
surface.

"Yes, sir," I sang out. Could I have already
advanced to the print shop?

"Take this bucket of solvent, see, and scrub out
all the old ink from the letters. Make 'em shine."

I loved my new job. I wanted to be the best
letter cleaner in the whole plant. I twisted the
corner of a rag like I was preparing to clean out
my ears and dipped the tip into the solvent. I
wiped the excess off on the lip of the bucket; I
didn't want to get sloppy. Then I worked the
nubbin of cloth around each crevice of each
character. Forty-five minutes later I had finished
six letters. I stepped back to admire my work.
"Fine, really fine."

Just then the foreman returned. "Hey, Johnson,
what the deuce are you doin'?" he shouted.

"I've got six letters done," I announced with
pride as if I had just lost my virginity.

"You college know-it-all's."

I could tell by his tone of voice that he was
not paying homage to my scholastic savvy.

"Gimme that rag," he said. The foreman dunked
cloth and fist into the solvent and then sloshed the
rag across the press like a maniac. Solvent, sweat,
and spit splattered like shrapnel. It was awesome.
In three strokes the entire press was glistening.
He turned, looked at me with disgust, and made a

disparaging choo-choo sound. Three days later I was fired.

I don't know; was it my fault? My intentions were honorable, but my knowledge was lacking. I think what I needed at the time was a mentor, a wise and loyal adviser to get me over the hump. After all, even the most self-sufficient of us can benefit from the guidance of a good friend — someone like Murray.

Years later — long after my short stint at the paper mill — I was teaching at a community college in Oregon. Murray was one of the first people I met; we became friends almost immediately. I was intrigued by his devotion to the fine arts. He loved Shakespeare, the Romantic poets, and the purest of classical music, particularly Brahms. It was this latter interest that captivated me.

I had always been drawn to classical music but had little understanding of it. There were a few pieces I liked: Wagner's "Ride of the Valkyries," Debussy's "Clair de Lune," Chopin's "Prelude in E minor" — all selections which were immediately appealing. But I can't say that I understood them. I knew nothing about the periods, the structure of music, and even less about the composers. But I wanted to learn.

One day I asked Murray if he would share his knowledge of classical music with me. Right away I knew that I had struck a chord. His eyes widened with delight. "I would like that very much," he said.

We agreed to meet at his home once a week. On each occasion we discussed a period of music, the key composers, and the most influential works. Then Murray would play several recordings, explaining the structure and innovations of each piece.

Those sessions were wonderful. All week I looked forward to that time when Murray and I would explore the magic of another musical masterpiece. I will never forget those evenings. Murray had become my musical mentor, introducing me to the world of Bach, Beethoven, and, of course, Brahms.

To this day, whenever I listen to the power of a Mahler symphony or the gentleness of a Chopin nocturne, I think to myself, "Thank you, Murray; you were the best."

Whenever I think about the foreman at the paper mill, I think . . . of something else.

A MILE DOWN THE ROAD at the edge of a cherry orchard, stands a grand old cottonwood tree. It is powerful and big, maybe four stories high and equally broad. It would take three grown men with arms outstretched to circumscribe its craggy, elephant-hide trunk. Through the years that granddaddy of a tree has gobbled up a metal fence post and a rusty line of barbed wire. The wire pokes out from its trunk like twisted cat whiskers.

Last summer my father-in-law, John Astleford, a retired Quaker missionary, stood under the shade of that old giant and thought the thoughts of a seventy-six-year-old man. Perhaps he reflected on the events of 1962 on the plains of Guatemala, his home for 35 years.

John was 39 years old at the time. The Presbyterian church in Guatemala City had invited him to speak to their congregation. It was a four-hour journey, but John was more than happy to serve.

An hour into the trip, John stopped at the toll booth at the entrance of the Pan American highway. Two young men approached his Chevrolet carryall.

"Please help us," they pleaded. "Our mother is dying, and we must go to her. It is Holy Week and all the buses are overcrowded. Please, sir, would you be kind enough to give us a ride?"

Naturally, John invited the travelers to join him. They drove for over two hours. During that time John shared his faith with the two men. Finally, John pulled off to the side of the road. "This is your stop," he said.

"Just a little farther," one of the men said. "Down that dirt road."

A few minutes later the other man spoke. "That is good," he said. "Right here, please."

John stopped the carryall and turned to say goodbye to the two men. He was about to say *vaya con Dios* when he turned and found himself staring into the barrel of a revolver. John watched the man squeeze down on the trigger. The first bullet entered his right cheek, shattering his teeth and exploding the roof of his mouth. The second bullet grazed the back of his neck. Quickly, the two men shoved him under the dash. Incredibly, John remained conscious; he could hear them talking.

"Keep looking," one of them said frantically. "He is an American. He must have a lot of money."

Moments later the two men were gone. John managed to right himself in the seat. He pulled a hand towel from the glove compartment and pressed the cloth against the gaping hole on the side of his face.

Somehow he managed to drive twenty kilometers to the American Hospital in Guatemala City. Two nurses were coming off duty when he arrived. Quickly, they half walked, half carried the bleeding man to emergency.

John, still conscious, motioned for a pencil and paper. What would he write? "I have no mouth?" "Tell my family I love them?" No. These were the words he scrawled. "My name is John Astleford. Please tell the Presbyterian church I will not be able to fulfill my commitment."

Sometime later John was scheduled to see the plastic surgeon to begin reconstructive surgery on the roof of his mouth. But there was no work to be done. Inconceivably, the gap had closed on its own! The surgeon, a man of science, was beside himself. He jumped back, ran to the door, flung it open, and screamed to his nurses. "Look at this!" he exclaimed. "It is a miracle! My God, it is a miracle!"

Perhaps John thought about those days while standing under the shade of the old cottonwood tree. Maybe he identified with that grand old wooden tower. Perhaps he said to the tree, "I know you old man. You have enveloped wire and stake, as my body has enveloped bone and teeth and lead. We are living testimonies of God's miraculous ways, you and I."

No, John would not say that; it is too boastful and much too dramatic. He is a man unfamiliar with pride and devoid of pretense — a man as solid as a cottonwood, but as meek as the evening summer breeze.

LAST SUMMER I solved a thirty-two-year-old mystery. It was thirty-two years ago that my best friend walked out on me. His name was David. Both of us were twelve years old.

David and I were inseparable. My mother used to call us "Mutt and Jeff." When I decided to be a little league pitcher, David trained to be a catcher. When David delivered the *Tri-City Herald* after school, I tagged along and practiced my sinker, chucking the news in the general direction of the customer's front door. The two of us were blood brothers—literally; we sealed our friendship with a hunting knife, a slice of thumb, and the inter-mingling of blood.

We did that the same night I got caught with my pants down. It was midsummer. David and I had decided to camp out in his back yard. There we were in our sleeping bags, side by side, staring at the underbelly of the moon and stars. It was a night for adventure.

"I dare you," David said again.

"You can't dare me. I dared you first."

"Yeah, but you're the oldest."

"What does that have to do with it?"

"I dunno; it just seems important."

There was a certain logic to his argument, so I decided to go for it. I slipped off my tee-shirt, squirmed out of my shorts and blasted out of my bag like a wild badger on the attack.

"Gerrronimo!" I shouted, bolting around the neighbor's house in a thin cloak of goose bumps and sweat, my arms and legs pumping for home. I rounded the last corner and executed the perfect baseball slide into the sack.

David was next. He also shouted "Geronimo." I think it's the universal battle cry for careening around a neighbor's house in the buff. I also think it was our undoing.

The next morning David's mom—stalwart of the Baptist church—called us into the kitchen. She did not raise her voice, but her words cut to the heart. "Allen, I'm disappointed in you. I thought you were better than that."

It was years before I could look the woman in the eyes again. I always had the unsettling feeling that she was picturing my little dingus twirling in the breeze.

Such misadventures could only happen with David. You don't think up stuff like that with a casual friend—only with a blood brother.

But then something happened. In the fall of seventh grade, David disappeared. Oh, he still lived in the same house just down the street, but I never saw him any more. We no longer walked to school in the morning, played catch in the afternoon, or did our homework at night. Those days were gone.

I felt a great emptiness that fall. I felt like someone had reached into my body, grabbed my heart, and squeezed the blood out of it. Still, I did not know why.

The mystery was unsolved until I saw David at our twenty-fifth high school reunion. I swear, he looked the same: blond, boyish, with that same winning smile.

"I want to talk to you," he said.

"Me too."

The music was blaring so we stepped out of the hotel banquet room and into the hall.

"Allen," he said, "I want you to know what happened when we were kids — why I drifted away."

I felt my heart quicken.

"You remember both of us were pretty religious in those days, going to church services three times a week."

"I remember."

"At that time you were a symbol of everything that was holy for me, a kind of beacon for the church."

"I never felt much like a beacon," I thought to myself.

"But I wanted to experiment. I wanted to see what the other side was like, the worldly side. I could only do that by divorcing myself from you. Of course, I could never walk away from the church, it was too much a part of me, but I didn't know that then. Do you understand?"

"Yes," I said, my eyes filling with tears. "I had no idea."

"I know that. What I did was cruel. I just cut you off. I knew that hurt, but I didn't know any other way to do it. Allen, I'm sorry. I'm truly, truly sorry."

"Give me a hug, David. I could really use a hug right now."

And the two of us embraced — two old little leaguers, grabbing hold of each other with the passion of thirty-two years of separation.

It was tough being a twelve-year-old with a yearning for the ways of the world, but David handled that passage, and many others, with indisputable success — learning to welcome each transition as a signpost that he was maturing as a compassionate human being.

You're looking good blood brother. (You want to take a naked dash around the neighbor's house?)

THIS IS HELEN'S STORY. It begins during the Great Depression. She was the daughter of Greek immigrants, struggling to make a life for themselves in the New World. Helen's father, Tony, owned a small diner in the heart of Philadelphia. Her mother, Katherine, was a seamstress, working twelve hours a day, six days a week in a dress factory on the other side of town.

Every Monday morning Katherine took her pretty three-year-old daughter to a Greek boarding house where she roomed for the week. That was the routine.

Then, one cold Saturday night, Katherine discovered the child was missing. Incredibly, the house matron told the young mother that her daughter had died during the week. But that didn't make any sense. Helen was a healthy child; and where was the body?

With time the matron's story unraveled. The
woman had actually sold the black-eyed infant to a
Greek priest for two hundred dollars under the
pretense that the child had been abandoned.

When Tony and Katherine learned the truth,
they went to court. Two trials and one year later,
they had won. It was the child's sixteen-year-old
brother who turned the case. When he was called
to the stand, he called out to his sister in her
Greek name. Helen ran to her brother and wrapped
her arms around his neck. The reunion was enough
to sway the court.

As strange as that story is, it does not end
there. Two years later the marriage of Tony and
Katherine ended in a brutal divorce. Without a
word to her ex-husband, Katherine took Helen and
fled to New York. But she soon lost heart and was
unable to keep the family together. She began to
look for an orphanage for her daughter. Helen
passed in and out of three institutions, finally
settling in the Kallman Home, a city orphanage in
Brooklyn, New York. She was six years old and
would spend the next twelve years at Kallman.

Those were not bad years for Helen. The
Lutheran minister who ran the home was strict, but

caring. True, it was often a struggle to keep the orphanage solvent; sometimes the children would produce a short play to help raise money for the home. Breakfast was always the same, mush. And Christmas was limited to one new present—a harmonica, a baseball, a small doll—donated by charitable organizations within the city.

But despite that lean existence, Helen always felt accepted and loved. Every second Sunday, on visiting day, her mother arrived, sometimes with candy or Greek cookies, and they would chat in the play room for two or three hours. But Katherine never spoke about Tony, and that was a sadness for Helen. She had fond memories of her father and yearned to see him again.

When Helen was eighteen, she left Kallman Home. She worked on an assembly line at a Western Electric plant in New Jersey during the war. Every morning she went to the same restaurant for breakfast. On one of those mornings, an amazing thing happened. Helen overheard the waiter talking with another customer.

"I went to a swell party in Philadelphia," he said. "Great food and plenty of booze. Except the host, this Greek fella, was really sad. For the last ten years he's spent a pile of dough searching for his lost daughter."

"What was the man's name?" Helen asked.

"Marco, Tony Marco."

Helen's head jerked back. "That's my father."

That day father and daughter were reunited. It was a tearful and joyous reunion, but not without conflict. Tony was quite wealthy now and had remarried. His new wife, Elsie, was immediately suspicious and jealous of the intruder. Helen quickly recognized that she was a threat to the woman, so she decided to leave.

Ten years later Helen was married and living on the West Coast. During those years she had faithfully written to her father, but never received a single response. She imagined that he no longer cared. What she did not know was that Elsie had intercepted and destroyed every letter. It took ten years and a private investigator for Tony to discover the truth. When Elsie was found out, Tony divorced her and the second ten-year reunion between father and child was arranged.

With a story like that, you might have expected Helen to have become an embittered woman. After all, the cards were stacked against her. She was shuffled around, raised in an orphanage, blocked from her father. By all rights she should be a miserable woman. Those who whine about being a victim of their unfortunate past would not disagree.

Yet, this woman is undoubtedly the kindest, most loving person I know. She is gentle and sensitive. She is a counselor for the distraught and an advocate for the oppressed. She is also an incredible mother. I should know; this woman, Helen Marco Johnson, graduate of the Kallman Home for orphaned children, is my mom.

I WONDER IF ALL CHILDREN SUFFER this
way? When I was twelve years old, I went through
a period when I thought nobody liked me. I don't
know why I felt that way; I was not an unpopular
kid. I held a post on the crosswalk patrol, received
my share of punch-out valentine cards, and even
filled a term as president of classroom 101.

And, yet, I still felt blue. I would lie in my
bed in the middle of the day, staring blankly at my
model airplanes strung from the ceiling overhead
and wonder about the meaning of it all. It was a
heavy burden for a twelve-year-old to carry.

"I feel so unhappy," I told my mother one day.

"Oh, son, what's wrong?" she asked, holding my
face in her warm, soft hands.

"I don't know." I was on the verge of tears;
one more question and I would be sobbing. "I just
feel empty and sad," I said quivering.

My mother comforted me as best she could, but it was not enough to soothe my tender sorrows. I was beginning to think that I would never be happy again when something occurred that shook me to the core.

It happened after school. A bunch of us were playing flag football on the school playground. We were laughing and snorting and crashing to the ground like wounded elephants. For a moment I had forgotten my sadness.

It was dusk. Suddenly, in the middle of an end run, a flash of jagged white light ruptured the sky. At the same instant, there was the unmistakable sound of electricity, crackling like cross-wired jumper cables. It was as though ten thousand flash bulbs fired all at once.

We were not looking at the sky, but we all saw it. It was not lightning; there were no clouds overhead. It was not the flash of the setting sun on a window pane or metal shingle. It was nothing like that.

Fifty yards away, at the top of a high school stadium light tower, a man hung from a single cord attached to his belt. He was bent over backwards, his arms and legs limply dangling below his head.

His face was blackened from the electrical charge. A wild cable snapped and popped like a snake striking and recoiling and striking again. We knew he was dead. A few minutes later another man climbed the tower and gently eased his partner down with a hand line.

No one dared to speak. We walked home quietly, solemnly, absorbed in our own thoughts. I could not stop picturing the lineman grotesquely suspended overhead.

I had never seen a dead man before. It seemed inconceivable to me that a man could be alive one moment and gone the next. I was bewildered by the frailty of life. "It is so short," I said to myself, "and so quickly gone."

You might think that incident would have deepened my despair. It did not happen that way; the next morning my sadness had vanished. Somehow in the middle of the night, it had been replaced with a sense of respect and thanksgiving for life. That was the end of my brush with childhood depression, but not the end of my thoughts on the event.

I grieved for the man who died that fall afternoon. I still grieve for his family, wherever they may be. But I am convinced of this. That man — son or husband or father — did not die without meaning. In a way, the man on the tower gave his life for me.

IN THE SUMMER OF 1969, I was twenty-three years old. I had it all: a wife, a job, and a brand new, baby blue, two-seater, convertible 850 Fiat Spider. That car was my mechanical offspring — I used to dental floss the wire spokes, for Pete's sake. It was also my nemesis.

That summer my wife and I decided to drive across the United States, from the Pacific to the Atlantic — "from the mountains, to the prairies, to the ocean white with foam," — the ultimate test of man and machine!

The car blew up just outside of Denver.

There we were with a cracked block in a one-pump town and a mechanic who thought a Fiat Spider was an imported insect. Sure, there was a dealership in Denver, but we were determined to go east — no sissy turning back for us. Only the nearest easterly dealership was Omaha, Nebraska, some 500 miles away. The question was, how to get there.

Being on a tight budget, our first attempt was to hitch a ride on an empty, eastbound semi. No go; "Insurance companies wouldn't buy it," they told us.

Our next idea was to rent a truck and transport the car ourselves. So we hitchhiked 35 miles to the nearest U-Haul dealership and picked out the biggest truck they had. But when it came time to pay for the rental, I realized I had left my traveler's checks locked in the Fiat.

"Look," I said to the attendant, "I forgot my checks. Will you let me take the truck, load up the car, come back here, and pay you off?"

"I can't do that," he said matter-of-factly. "Besides, it's almost quittin' time. You'd never get back in time."

"Okay," I said, taking off my wrist watch, "this is a Rolex. Mr father gave it to me for high school graduation. Look, it's even engraved with my name. Keep it until I come back with your truck."

"I don't want your watch," he said blankly.

I looked at my wife. I was running out of

ideas. I turned back to him. "Take my wife."

"Huh?"

"You know I'm going to come back for my wife. We've only been married for six months; I'm not ready to give her up yet."

For some reason that seemed to do it. He agreed to keep my wife until I returned with the loaded U-Haul. Now, when I think about what I did, offering my wife to a strange man for collateral, I can hardly believe it. But we were young, and it seemed like the right thing to do at the time.

I used a cattle ramp to load the Fiat—I still don't know how I did that. It was in, but not *all* the way in; it stuck out in the back by about six inches. So I let out half the air in all four tires, pulled up the emergency brake to the last possible click, and roped off the back. "No fast starts," I kept telling myself.

It was ten o'clock by the time I returned to the U-Haul dealership. As it turned out, my wife had shared dinner with the attendant's family; the conversation had been polite, but a little strained. That was all right; we were on the road again.

That night we slept at a rest stop, my wife in

the cab of the truck, I in the back alongside the stupid Fiat.

The next morning we drove directly to the dealership in Omaha. The entire staff came out from cluttered desks and ailing cars to see the strange couple from Washington with their 850 Spider in the back end of a U-Haul truck. They looked amused, the way you look at a friend's baby who just broke wind. "Isn't that the cutest thing?"

They unloaded the car and put it on the rack. Yep, it was a cracked block, all right. They could fix it, but it would take two weeks to get the parts.

"Two weeks!" I squawked. "What are we going to do in Omaha, Nebraska, for two weeks?"

The mechanic stared back at me with that same amused look. "I don't rightly know," he said helpfully.

My wife and I walked to the showroom and plopped down. We wondered how we were going to survive for half a month in a strange town. We didn't have enough money for a hotel and meals, unless we wanted to hole up at the town mission. Our budget was precise; we had just enough cash to get from the home of one relative to the next. A two-week layover was not in our financial portfolio.

Then a strange thing happened. A tall, middle-aged man walked over to where we were huddled.

"Excuse me," he said. "My name is John. I overheard your predicament, and I wondered if I could help out. I'd be happy to have you stay with us while you're waiting to have your car repaired."

I didn't know what to say. "But-but it won't be fixed for two weeks," I finally stammered.

"So I understand," he said. "That's why I'd like to help."

I looked at my wife. "What do you think, honey?"

"It's fine with me," she said turning to John. "Are you sure it'll be okay with your wife?"

He smiled as though tickled by her concern. "Well, almost sure. But I'll call just in case."

A few minutes later, John came back. "Everything's cleared," he announced. "Shall we go?"

I felt somehow easier when we got into John's car, a charcoal grey Mercedes sedan. We drove for about ten minutes. The conversation was pleasant and natural; I liked him right away.

John's home was a showplace. It was a

modern, two-story house with lots of glass and vaulted ceilings. The back porch overlooked a virgin forest. I glanced at my wife who pursed her lips and whistled silently.

The next two weeks were a wonderful holiday. John was an artist; the walls of his home were lined with his abstract paintings. But primarily, he was a jeweler, a master at crafting beautiful, bold rings and pendants out of silver and gold.

John's wife, Linda, was equally talented, a sculptor with a fondness for clay and multi-colored glazes. She was also a teacher. In fact, while we were there, she prepared for a showing of her students' brightly-colored, three-dimensional collages. They looked like giant cutouts of Picasso paintings.

We covered a lot of ground in those fourteen days. We tinkered at making jewelry; we went to the movies; we did a little gardening around the house. Then we talked late into the night about great books and art and the mystery of life. When our car was finally repaired, we were actually disappointed.

The morning we left, I asked John why he had invited us —why he had taken the risk.

"For selfish reasons," he said smiling. "You seemed like an interesting couple, and I wanted the chance to get to know you."

That's all he said; it was that simple.

Twenty years later, they are still remembered. We remember their kindness, their vitality, their passion for people. After all the years, they still make perfect sense.

ERNIE WAS NEVER OLD. Even when he was old, he was young. He was the kind of man a boy wanted to go fishing with. He was gentle and a little mischievous.

He squinted his eyes like Clark Gable when he spoke to you, recounting wonderful stories about growing up, about stoking fires in the cold winters and making do on practically nothing — even less than nothing.

Then he would tell the hitchhiking story. Ernie had double-jointed thumbs; he could cock his thumb back like a hammer on a pistol. He said they got that way from hitchhiking so much. I was always pretty sure he was joking, but still a piece of me wondered if it might really be true.

I heard those stories plenty of times. I knew the tales about his sheriffing days. I could recit the adventures about running the big crane. But

the stories I loved most were the yarns about
delivering Western Union messages on the streets of
Seattle. He was just sixteen—not much older
than I—bicycling up and down the avenues and
alleys, darting in and out of traffic, living on the
edge of his seat.

"I was in shape then," he said, his eyes
squinting.

It was not a boast. Nor was it taken as a
boast; it was just a matter of fact. It was always
the last line to the Western Union story. When he
said, "I was in shape then," I knew the story was
over.

Ernie was Sunday school superintendent at our
church. Every Sabbath he was there, as regular as
the preacher. As a boy I was always intrigued by
his Sunday school attendance pin: a lapel cluster
the size of a quarter with a bar attached for every
year of perfect attendance. He had twelve or
thirteen bars, dangling like a ladder from the
Kingdom. It was splendid; I wanted a string of bars
just like it. Twice I got up to two years and then
I would come down with the flu, miss a Sunday, and
have to start all over again. It was discouraging.

But Ernie never missed. When I was a boy, I

thought he wore the pin for himself. When I grew up, I realized he wore it for us.

Ernie had a way of making a boy feel special. He sang tenor in the church choir and invited me to sing tenor too. I was really a baritone, but I wanted to sit next to Ernie more than I wanted to sing true. Every Sunday we sat side by side. I stood close and sometimes sang out just a hair behind Ernie when I wasn't sure of the pitch. He knew what I was doing; he just smiled and winked his Clark Gable wink.

When I first started to play trumpet, I wanted Ernie to hear my B-flat scale. I put the horn to my lips, curled my toes, and blew: "Do-re-mi-fa-sol-SPLAT-ti-do."

"That's fine," Ernie said, "really fine."

"But I can only go up the scale," I said. "I don't know how to go down yet."

"Sure you can," Ernie said. "Give it a try; you can do it."

And sure enough I *could* go down the scale: "Do-ti-la-sol-fa-mi-SPLAT-do."

Even now I remember that simple expression of belief in me.

I was a grown man when Ernie died. I was

asked to be a pallbearer at his funeral; it was a sad, but proud honor.

The services were held in the church where Ernie and I had sung tenor so many Sunday mornings. I felt as if the wind had been knocked out of me; a smile was unthinkable. Then I saw Ernie's daughter, Ruthelma. She was smiling serenely, almost glowing.

"He was so important to me," I told her.

"I know," she said. "Thank you for coming to celebrate with us."

Yes, to celebrate — that was the perfect expression. We were there to celebrate a man's contribution to humanity. We were there to remember how he had touched us all. In the solitude of my own thoughts, I thanked Ruthelma for shaking me out of my misery.

Then the preacher got up to say a few words, but I wasn't listening. I was offering my own eulogy to the man who was willing to enter the life of a twelve-year-old boy: to the best Western Union delivery boy that Seattle ever saw. Ride, Ernie, ride.

I WAS DRIVING ON I-5 IN SEATTLE. It was rush hour. Suddenly, my car quit running. There was no warning; it just stopped. I managed to drift to the side of the freeway without incident. I got out of the car, popped the hood, and looked inside. I had no idea what I was looking for — maybe a loose connection somewhere, something blatant. I poked around for a few minutes, knowing I wouldn't find anything. I hate to admit it, but I have mechanical dyslexia. I look at an engine and I see alphabet soup, all the little letters swimming around in Russian.

I got back into the car and sat there for a long time. I considered my options. A professional towing service was out of the question. I was in graduate school at the time, living in a one-bedroom, basement apartment with just enough money to cover my books for spring term, and not much more. My wife couldn't help; we had only

one car. I wouldn't call my next door neighbor on
a bet. He looked funny at me when I said "good
morning," darting into his apartment like a startled
woodchuck. And I certainly couldn't ask any of my
graduate professors. We had a thoroughly antiseptic
teacher-student relationship. Calling one of them
would be as pleasant as kissing my great aunt, the
sweaty one with pudgy fingers and fat lips.

Eventually, I realized that there was only one
person I could call. His name was Dave. He was
the pastor of a Quaker church in the north end of
Seattle. His availability, though, was not a function
of the church; it was his way of being.

From the beginning, I knew that there was
something unique about Dave. I noticed that his
eyes did not wander when he spoke to me. He
nodded, probed here and there, and talked freely of
noble ventures. I always felt at home with him.
Our view of the world was different; mine tended
to be somewhat cynical, his more forward-looking,
but that didn't seem to matter. I was okay the
way I was. In fact, I was okay *because* of the way
I was. I felt honored for my talents and respected
for my humanness.

So I called Dave that day my car broke down.

He came, and we towed it away. As I recall, it was
a minor problem, a blown fuse or something equally
obvious.

Dave invited me to dinner. That night I told
him about the mental sifting I had gone through
before calling him.

"I thought I had more friends," I said. And
with that, emotion grabbed me by the throat, and I
began to sob. I am not sure why. It may have
been for sadness. Or it may have been for joy, for
thankfulness that I had this one true friend, this
one person I could go to without embarrassment.

Dave is gone now. He was killed in a private
plane crash. He was too young, and I miss him a
great deal. But he has left me with many fine
memories: philosophical discussions, playful
bantering, heart-to-heart talks. But mostly he
provided me with a model. Not an idol — neither
of us would accept that — but a model for
perhaps the world's most unexercised resource:
human compassion.

MY WIFE AND I HAD STRUCK OUT for a
walk on the outskirts of town near the place where
the Yakima River merges with the Columbia. We
were having a good time racing each other on the
spine of the railroad track, picking up colorful
rocks and watching the industry of ants and bugs.
Then, about half a mile down the line, we saw a
dark figure waving at us.

"Hold up," he shouted.

There was a kind of desperation in his voice,
so we reversed our course and headed his way,
thinking he might be in some sort of trouble. The
man started running toward us. By the time he
reached us, he was panting heavily. He held up his
hand, a signal for us to wait while he caught his
breath.

"Please, have you seen a little boy about so
high?" he finally asked, slicing the air with his

open hand. His voice was trembling, filled with
worry.

"No, I'm sorry," I said. "You're the first person
we've seen all day, but we'll keep a sharp look out.
We'll send him . . ."

The man had already turned. He was
scrambling down the track, shouting his son's name,
"Jason, Jason, JASON!"

A moment later two small figures emerged from
the underbrush near the river.

"Hey, Dad!" one of them shouted.

The father pulled up with a jerk.

"You get you're little butt over here right
now," he screamed. The boy put his head down and
advanced slowly.

"Move it!" the man bellowed. When the
youngster got within arm's reach the father
snatched him by the collar, giving him a snap that
dropped the boy to his knees.

"Now you get yourself home," he barked.
"You're in big trouble mister. You haven't heard
the last of this yet."

"What a shame," I thought. All the young boy
saw was an angry man. He did not witness the
heart-felt anxiety that had been exposed to us.

He might have said, "Son, I love you; I care about what happens to you. We need to talk about safe boundaries for your explorations." Instead, his frustration masked his genuine concern.

When people are under stress, they will "fight" (like Jason's father) or "take flight." It is their anxiety-provoked backup style, their choice of battle stations. Those who tend to be assertive in times of calm will generally become demanding when under pressure. On the other hand, people who are more timid, believing that relationships are too fragile to endure conflict, will usually withdraw or give in when under fire.

I was feeling pretty righteous about my assessment of Jason's father: "He really should do something about that temper." A few hours later, I proved to myself that I relied on the same attacking backup style.

After our walk, I drove into town to exchange a set of guitar strings at the music shop.

"We don't take exchanges," I was told.

"But the set is unopened," I argued. "Plus I want to exchange this packet for a set that costs less; you can even keep the change."

"Nope, we don't do that," the shopkeeper said.

Then another customer spoke up.

"It says right here that the store does not take exchanges," she said pointing at a sign under the glass counter.

That's when I attacked. I turned on the woman and snapped at her like a cranky pit bull.

"Who invited you into this conversation?" I demanded.

She shriveled.

I did not gain anything in that volley. In fact, I probably lost a good deal of respect. And I know better. I should have said in an adult voice, "Excuse me, ma'am, this is a private conversation." In that way I would have expressed what was important to me without lambasting her.

What can I say? I goofed up. I let my take-no-prisoners backup style pull rank. In the end I walked out of the shop with the same set of guitar strings and the hint of a headache over my right eye.

That was the day Jason's father debated how many swats to give his son. Jason was scared, the shopkeeper was miffed, and the woman customer was left bleeding. I hope somebody had a good day.

IN THE DAYS between my freshman and sophomore years in college, I led the summer youth program at a large Presbyterian church in West Seattle. It was there that I met Mr. Bailey.

Mr. Bailey was a short, husky man with enough dryness in his humor to crease your pants. I could tell that he liked me. In fact, I suspect it was he who slipped a twenty-dollar bill in the church offering one Sunday for the "Allen Johnson Memorial Fund." That would be like him.

That fall I returned to school; I did not see Mr. Bailey for two years. It was during that time that he suffered a paralyzing stroke. He still got around with the aid of a wheelchair, but he was never quite the same again.

The most dramatic change was in his language. Before the stroke, profanity was never in Mr. Bailey's vocabulary. Strangely, after the stroke, the few expressions he could utter were all combinations of swear words.

I will never forget the first time I saw Mr. Bailey after his stroke. I had accepted an invitation to work at the church for another summer. On that first Sunday I was asked to sing a solo in the evening service. When I stood to sing, Mr. Bailey recognized me. Tears filled his eyes. He could not say my name; he could not wish me God's blessings. So he did the only thing he could do. He pointed his finger at me and said in a trembling voice, "Son-of-a-bitch."

I think it was the sweetest greeting I have ever received.

My friend recognized me with the only resources he had at his disposal. Understanding his condition, the indiscretion in church is forgiven, even relished.

I elect Mr. Bailey as spokesman for all the people in the world who have trouble expressing their affection—the people who choke up when they want to say, "I like you; will you be my friend?"; the hardy who resort to a slap-on-the-back or a slug-to-the-arm, as if to say, "Hey old buddy, old pal, how you doin' anyway?"; the awkward who hint at their affection through "funny" putdowns, teasing the people they like; the painfully shy who offer their praise to somebody else and hope it gets back to the right person. The approaches may be clumsy and sometimes misunderstood, but the intent is warm-hearted, and who can fault that?

Mr. Bailey is my kind of guy—fighting with all his might to salute an old friend. And if he must defame my birthright to do it, that's okay. I've been called worse; I just haven't enjoyed it as much.

THERE WERE SIX OF US. We had our sleeping bags pitched out in Jim Mullen's front yard, a kind of campout for the church junior boys. Six blocks away in the church basement, the junior girls were having a slumber party.

Our sacks were laid out in the shape of a star, our heads clustered in the center. It was the perfect arrangement for whispered ghost stories: "Whoooo stole my goOOolden arm?"

We scared the begeebees out of each other for a good hour.

"Well, what d'ya wanna do now?" someone asked.

"I don't know. What do you wanna do?" I countered.

"Gee, I dunno."

The conversation was too much for Jerry. He wasn't any older than the rest of us, just thirteen, but always a little more daring. "Will you guys shut up?" he hollered. "I've got an idea. Why don't we see what the girls are doing?"

Suddenly, none of us had eyelids. Visit the girls?! Wow, the possibilities were galactic—but crazy. It was already close to midnight; if anyone ever found out, we'd be goners. Still, the more we thought about it, the more sensible it seemed.

In fact, after awhile, we figured we'd be nuts *not* to go. We began to visualize the scene: girls running around in scanty underwear, baiting us with suggestive giggles. (I knew about scanty underwear; I had seen it all in the front section of the Sears and Roebuck catalog.) No, there was no other way; the image was irresistible.

We slipped out of our bags and over the fence. For six blocks we ran with our heads down and our shoulders hunched. Then one of us yelled, "Car!" and we scrambled behind the nearest bush or garbage can. We were great—the "Dirty Half Dozen."

I can't remember how long it took us; time was not a factor. We would have crawled on our bellies to complete the mission.

Then we were there. We tapped on the

basement church windows. We heard giggling. A
window popped open, and the junior girls' Sunday
school teacher thrust her head through the opening.
Holy Toledo! None of us had thought about her.

"What do you boys think you're doing?" she
snapped.

What a dumb question; how should we know?
So we did the only thing we could do. We ran like
hell, six blocks, nonstop—wildmen with our pants
on fire—over the fence and into our sacks, and
fervently prayed for divine intervention.

The next morning, after the news hit the
Associated Press, my mother grabbed me by the ear
and escorted me to the car and impending doom.
"What were you thinking of?" she demanded.

What could I say? The truth? "Uh, well, mom,
I was thinking of breasts, and bottoms, and ladies
underwear." Not on your life! So I said what
every kid mutters when trapped by a puny argument
and the wish to continue living: "Gee, mom, I
dunno."

If I had known then what I know now, I might
have been more convincing: "Well, mom, it's really
quite straightforward when you stop to think about
it. You've heard the expression, *Be careful what*

you wish for; you might just get it? Well, that's
exactly what happened. The guys just started to
fantasize about girls—not just casually, mind
you, but in glorious Technicolor. So you see, it
was the power of visualization that propelled us to
jump the fence. We simply followed the lead of our
imagination. How can you fault that? Surely you
would not want to deprive us of our capacity for
imagination."

Do you think she would have bought that?
Nah! Her comeback would have been brutal: "I've
got your imagination on the end of this willow
switch. Drop 'em, buster."

If there is one thing I have learned, it is this:
It's impossible to use logic on a mother with a
weapon in her hand and malice in her heart.

I WAS EATING HOT AND SPICY Chinese food at the Stardust Hotel in Las Vegas. It tasted like confetti with extra pepper. Of course, you don't go to Las Vegas to eat; you go to Las Vegas to gamble. Eating is what you do to stay alive at the crap table.

I was almost done when I spotted a cigarette girl with high heels and towering legs on the other side of the room. I couldn't remember ever seeing a cigarette girl before, except in the movies. She actually announced in a husky, saloon voice, "Cigarettes, cigars, Tiparillos." She also sold yo-yos, one of which lit up like a spiraling neon rotor when she flipped it from her hand to the ground and back again. I was mesmerized. Up and down I watched the dazzling cylinder glide unencumbered from ankle to thigh. Gulp.

I was so engrossed by the spectacle that I

popped my fortune cookie into my mouth without
thinking. I chewed full gallop until I suddenly
realized I was eating my fortune. I discreetly
worked the dispatch forward, easing the paper out
between my front teeth with thumb and forefinger.
For a moment I looked like a human ticker-tape
machine. The snippet of paper was soggy but
decipherable:

Your fantasies are imaginative but honorable.

"Whoa!" I said out loud. Had some Chinese guy
read my mind? Or, worse, was my wife in the
kitchen, stuffing all fortune cookies with the same
bulletin? Impossible. Although I did glance over
my shoulder just to be on the safe side.

There was wisdom in that cryptic message. My
fantasies are often imaginative and, for the most
part, honorable—even in Las Vegas. I like my
fantasies. They are my friends. Why? Because
they help me to get what I want or release what I
can't have.

It is true that your fantasies, the images you
picture in your head, are a prerequisite to
achievement. They are the blueprints of your
desires. Nothing is accomplished unless these
fantasies are indulged.

Sometimes, however, people entertain negative fantasies. For example, they dream about hurting others by getting even. This is garbage thinking. They forget that "what goes around, comes around." In the end, they feel more miserable than ever.

The best way to end these negative fantasies is to allow them to flutter through your consciousness unimpeded. You may think of them as a bird flying directly through a house, in one window and out another. Wrestling with these bleak thoughts is another way of dwelling on them—giving them honor. They do not deserve the attention. My wife once said it as well as any: "It is the mark of a whole person to know which fantasies to run with."

I once met a young man who agonized about his sexual fantasies. He thought they were vile and depraved. "How can I think such awful thoughts?" he asked.

I advised the young man to relax. I suggested he could be more like my friend who enjoys reading *Playboy* magazine. One day his wife asked him how he could read "such filth."

His answer was simple. "I read *Playboy* for the same reason that I read *National Geographic.* It takes me to places I ain't ever gonna see otherwise."

That little bit of humor was a way of reframing the problem. What I was trying to say was this. "Hey, it's not that serious. If your fantasies distress you, let them go. Like my friend with the *Playboy*, look at the pictures and then set it aside. The child inside of us is curious about such things; there is nothing wrong with that. Satisfy your curiosity and then move on."

There may be some men who could look at a Las Vegas cigarette girl with incredible legs and lose a good night's sleep (I felt a whiff of insomnia myself), but one could do worse. The fantasy could come true, and how much fun would it be, tied spread-eagle to the bedposts with yo-yos.

JON WAS AWAKENED BY THE SOUND of his three-year-old son Scott crying in his room. He opened one eye, peering hopefully at his wife. Nope, she was konked out for the night. Half asleep, Jon rolled out of bed and shuffled to his son's room.

Scott was sobbing uncontrollably and babbling, "My leg. I-I-I lost my leg."

Jon guessed that his son was having a nightmare, so he tried to awaken him gently. "Son, wake up," he said softly. "Wake up, Scott; you're having a bad dream."

But Scotty *was* awake and sobbing harder than ever. "I lost m-m-my leg," he cried, barely able to get the words out.

Jon squelched his temptation to laugh. "Well, Son," he said, stroking the boy's head, "what makes you think you've lost your leg?"

With that Scott pealed back the blanket that covered his little body. And there it was. "LOOK!" he screamed. Scotty clutched an empty pajama pant leg in his fist, waving the flannel "flag" in horror.

At that point Jon *did* laugh. Somehow, in the middle of the night, little Scotty had managed to stuff both limbs into a single leg of his roomy pajama bottoms. For a moment, it looked for all the world as though he *had* lost his leg.

It is funny how a child can scare himself silly over the most innocuous event. And, yet, when it comes to creative misery, children have no monopoly on the market. To tell the truth, I think adults have come up with some real doozies. Here are some of my favorites.

Nocturne Willies. It is the middle of the night. Suddenly I hear a strange scratching noise. I immediately clench all my toes and imagine that a depraved maniac has escaped from the state penitentiary. Of all the houses in the world, he has chosen mine to violate. I envision that he has a particular perverted fondness for citizens of my precise temperament and body shape. But I refuse to investigate. I might discover the noise was only the cat seeking entry, and that would mess up a perfectly good misery.

Spider Phobia. I am working quietly at my desk. Out of the corner of my eye, I spot a spindly spider surreptitiously stealing up the wall. This is the perfect moment to create a flaming phobia. I instantly imagine that the hairy beast is a rare and deadly arthropod, capable of disguising itself as an innocent daddy-longlegs. The monster is equipped with an internal radar system that tracks humans with loose-fitting garments. It is able to pounce from here to Miami, careen down my shirt, and nest in my navel where it will multiply and order out for pizza. I decide to freak out.

Keeping Up the Front. I am taking an entitled Sunday afternoon nap when the telephone rings. Because my voice sounds a little groggy, the caller asks if I were sleeping. Ah-hah, the sterling opportunity to be miserable and make the intruder the unwitting villain. "No, I was just rereading a journal article on the renaissance of Aristotelian philosophy." This is an artful dodge. In one well-formed sentence I have achieved three outcomes: (a) guilt for lying about being awake, (b) shame for pretending to be more scholarly than William F. Buckley, and (c) misery for allowing the imagined opinions of the caller to rule my life. Wow! A three-banger!

Misery through Alienation. This is a dating game tactic I discovered in Dan Greenburg's delightful book, *How to Make Yourself Miserable.* It is characterized by the suitor's appeal for rejection. With minor variations, the dialogue twitches along like this.

Allen:	You probably have something better to do, so I guess you wouldn't want to, like, go to movies on Friday night.
Mary:	As a matter of fact, I have nothing planned for next Friday.
Allen:	So it would be like scraping the bottom of the bucket to go with me, right?
Mary:	I didn't say that.
Allen:	But that's what you meant.
Mary:	(Hesitantly.) No, not at all. But now that I think about it, I do have a lot going on this weekend.
Allen:	Sure, kick me while I'm down; I'm used to it. I must have been crazy to think you would actually go out with me anyway. I hope you and your

jillion fans will be very happy
together.

Beautiful. I have managed to deprecate myself
and insult Mary at the same time. This is a
powerful technique. Both of us should be miserable
for at least two to three days.

Well, there they are: my all-star misery lineup.
Understand that this has been an extremely short
course in the art of adult miserablizing. The
techniques are, after all, as prolific as human
inspiration. One guy I know is persuaded that the
bank teller deliberately slows down when he gets in
line. Another acts as though the "jerk" who cut
him off in traffic was following him for weeks,
waiting for just that opportunity to burn his shorts.
I even met a woman at a picnic who took personal
responsibility for a turn in the weather.

I realize all this stuff sounds pretty silly —
kind of like losing a leg in the middle of the night.
Still, with a little effort I can make myself
perfectly crazy — or perfectly sane. One way or
the other, it's all in my head — and not up my
sleeve.

MY BRUSH WITH THE DEVIL is the name of this story.

It happened in Algeria. My wife and I were living in a big two-story, stucco house that once sheltered Berber resistance fighters during the country's war of independence with the French. It was an old house and a little bit haunted. The ghosts of Algerian soldiers held up in the attic at night and made plans for the battle at dawn. I know they were ghosts; I looked.

One cold winter night, my wife nudged me in the ribs.

"Allen, are you awake?" she whispered.

"I am now," my voice rumbled.

"Listen," she breathed. "I think there's someone in the attic."

"No, it's just the wind," I told her. "Go back to sleep."

I rolled over on my side and closed my eyes. Then I opened my eyes. What was that? It sounded like someone walking directly overhead. Thump, thump, thump. There *was* someone in the attic — or something. I had to find out.

"I'm going up," I said resolutely.

"You can't go up there," my wife gasped. "What if they thump you on the head?"

Good question. Still I had to look. I am like that; I have to see to believe. But more than that, I *want* to see so I *can* believe. But I'm getting ahead of myself.

I got a step ladder from downstairs and set it up under the lid that covered the access to the attic. I climbed silently up the ladder and pushed the lid up and to one side. Then slowly — veeerry slowly — I eased my head through the opening, breaking the thin film that separates the real world from ghost country. In one quick movement, my head swiveled 360 degrees. Yep, ghosts all right. Had to be; no one else was there. That makes sense, doesn't it? If it isn't organic, it must to be supernatural.

(Later I wondered what I would have said if there had been a live person holed up in the attic.

"Ah, excuse me. I hope I'm not bothering you, but could you hold it down up here? My wife and I are trying to get a little sleep, if you don't mind.")

The scene was set for my visit with the devil. A couple of nights later I was reading a novel that a friend had sent to me from the states, *The Exorcist*. This is not a happy book and not a volume I recommend to my friends. But in 1974 *Time* magazine ran a big story on the frenzy generated by the movie. I decided to see for myself what all the hullabaloo was about.

That night I read the spooky part about the little girl and the bed that shook and rattled and spun around. That was enough for me. I set the book on the night table, turned off the light and went to sleep. Then, just before dawn, *my* bed started shaking, the metal frame chattering on the hardwood floor like a loose shingle in the wind.

Every muscle in my body marbleized; you could have used me for a javelin. I kept thinking, "The devil's after me. That must be it. I don't know what I said or what I did, but he wants me." And then I thought, "Wait a minute, maybe *God* wants me. Yeah, maybe God has this really neat idea, and I'm tangled up in it somehow."

So there in the morning light I waited to hear either the voice of God or the voice of the devil.

Waiting . . . until, "Honey!"

Who's that? "Honey" seemed too casual for God and too affectionate for the devil.

"Honey, we just had an earthquake."

It was my wife. I knew it was she; I could see her lips moving. And I was still on earth and alive and attached to my soul. Sure, it all made sense now. It was just an earthquake; they had those things in this part of the country. Very logical.

And yet just seconds before, I was convinced that I was traded to the devil. How could I have thought that? I'm so rational, so objective about stuff like that. How could I be so quickly swayed?

I am not sure what I believe about spiritual things. But I do believe that our cynicism should be carefully governed. If we can so quickly believe that there is a ghost in the attic or a devil under the bed, then we can also believe, as I think we do, that there is a source of goodness, there, somewhere, just beyond our sight but well within our reach.

I THOUGHT I WAS ON A ROLL. My jokes
were working, my examples were dramatic, and the
faces in the audience were all plugged in. All, that
is, except for one. A man in the middle of the
auditorium sat with his arms folded, his legs
crossed, and his eyes wanning like two pale moons
rising, rising . . . gone. He wasn't ugly, just
miserable.

I notice those things. I don't know—call me
funny that way—I can tell when someone would
rather be in Cleveland. So I decided to confront
the man.

"Excuse me, sir. I get the feeling that you're
not really buying any of this. Are you willing to
share with me what's going on?" You'll notice that
I did not say, "Pardon me, but have you recently
passed away?"

The man was not afraid to speak up. His words

were simple and to the point. "I don't like what you're saying, and I don't like the way you're saying it."

The crowd of about 150 raised and lowered their eyebrows in unison. My scalp shifted about an inch and a half to the west.

"Gee," I finally said, "if you're not finding any of this helpful, please feel free to leave."

"I can't," he droned. "I'm with a car pool, and I'm stuck here for the next two hours."

So there he sat through the rest of the seminar, Chief Bump-on-a-Log, defying me to say anything remotely interesting.

That happens every so often. In fact, in a crowd of that size, you can usually expect to find one or two faces that have retired for the evening.

Rejection! Like most everyone, I've had my share: the final cut from the basketball squad, the botched job interview, and—heartache of heartaches—the kiss-off from my college sweetheart.

"I'm looking for somebody more sensitive," she said gently.

"I can be sensitive."

"Yeees, but I also want a man who's rugged."

"I can be rugged. You want rugged? I'll be rugged."

"Uh, I'm really looking for . . . somebody else."

"I CAN BE SOMEBODY ELSE! WHO DO YOU WANT ME TO BE?"

With time I have grown to accept the fact that rejection is part of living. Really, when I think about it—when my head is cool and my passions tempered—I wouldn't want it any other way. For me to ask for a world without rejection is to demand a world without choices. And who wants that? People have the capacity—and right— to make their own selections; that's just the way it is.

One final example to make my point. Included in our natural right of selection is the freedom to choose our own professional title.

A few years ago, a woman delivered our mail. One Saturday morning I happened to glance out the window as she was walking toward our front door.

"Here comes the mailman," I announced to my wife without thinking.

"Not a mailman," she corrected, "a mailperson."

I'm a fast learner, so I sprung open the door and chortled, "Gooood morning, mailperson."

I knew right away that I had said something wrong. She shot me a look usually reserved for child molesters and mother rapers.

"I'm a letter carrier!" she barked indignantly.

That's all she said. She turned on her heels, and reeled off in search of more deserving mail slots.

I was left with my mouth open and my index finger drooping in midair. "Gee, what'd I say?"

Rejected again.

I've learned my lesson — the mailman is now a letter carrier. But if a letter carrier should suddenly become a "mail escort," I will not be surprised, nor will I fall apart if my ignorance is met with displeasure. In the end, my status as a fully functioning human being is not contingent on approval or rejection by others — members of the audience, lovers, letter carriers — it is contingent on the approval and selection of myself.

WHEN I WAS DATING IN HIGH SCHOOL, midnight was the bewitching hour. I knew that if I unlocked the latch to the front door on the morning of the next day, my life would be in great jeopardy. That was understood. The rule seemed fair enough to me; so I consented, and there was peace and goodwill in the household. Except once.

One Friday night I lost track of time. My date and I were at a friend's house. It was all very innocent. The four of us sprawled out in front of the fireplace, munched on popcorn, and asked the important questions: "Can you imagine an infinite universe?" "Would you rather be wise and miserable, or naive and happy?" "Is it polite to make armpit noises in mixed company?" You know, all the really important stuff.

Then I looked at my watch; it was two-thirty in the morning. I did not know how that happened

——I'm still not sure——but I did know I was in deep trouble.

I drove my date home in record time. Then, half a block from my house, I turned off the lights and engine and coasted to a stop at the front curb. That's when I saw it. THE LIGHTS WERE STILL ON. I had a small post-pubescent heart attack. This was not going to be easy.

I got out of the car and walked the last steps of the condemned. I was halfway to the front stoop when the front door flew open. My mother loomed silhouetted in the doorway. I knew it was Mom; I recognized the fire and smoke. Immediately, she launched into the WORRIED MOTHER'S SPEECH.

"How dare you come home at this hour? What kind of son are you? I thought I raised you better than that. Staying out all hours of the night. Don't you EVER do that again! Do you hear me?"

I wasn't sure if the question was rhetorical, so I started to answer.

"Don't you talk back to me," she snapped, a little pause between each word for dramatic emphasis. "I was worried to death. For all I knew you could have been dead in a ditch some place."

It flashed through my mind that my demise was always "in a ditch someplace"—as though that were the only place on earth where a teenager could die. That seemed a little funny to me, but I didn't think it was the right time to challenge her logic.

The speech continued, but you get the idea.

I learned two things that night. First, not to be late. But more important, I learned that I had control of my mother's emotions. If I wanted to make my mom crazy (which I didn't), all I had to do was to stay out a little past midnight. I had the power to make Mom sick with worry. And if that was correct, the reverse was also true: Mom had the power to make *me* sick or worried or angry or depressed.

Although this kind of thinking is often unconscious, it is, nevertheless, flawed. It is based on the notion that all of us are victims of circumstances; something we dislike happens, and we have no other alternative but to fall to pieces. It doesn't work that way; there is a middle step. Events in themselves don't control our emotions; our *interpretation* of the events do that. When a son comes home late from a date, parents have a choice. They can decide to be miserable —based on their interpretation of the event —or they can decide to deal with the problem.

Coming home late is not a problem I have any more. (I get sleepy every night around ten o'clock.) But if I were uncommonly late one night, and my wife exceedingly distraught, I might pose this gentle question: "I'm okay, honey; what have you been telling yourself tonight?"

ONE SUMMER NIGHT I had the terrific honor of speaking at a local high school graduation ceremony. Well, it wasn't really a ceremony; it was more like a festival. The stadium rang with hoops and hollers and cat whistles; high-fives were popping all over the place.

It was nothing like my high school graduation. Back then we were stiff and stoic, accepting our diplomas like knighthood from the Queen of England. In contrast, last night felt more like a Greek wedding at Mardi gras. No one was waiting for permission to have a good time.

I like this new spirit of celebration. I love the sharing of human emotion: the joy, the anticipation, the pride, the tinge of sadness. It is all there, transparent and real.

At the end of the program, after the names were called, after the mortarboards were flung, after the balloons were released and the fireworks discharged—after all that, I did not want to leave. I stood on the small stage and watched 3000 people storm the field.

I saw a fourteen-year-old boy with a punk hairdo wipe his eyes with the tail of his tee shirt. At first I thought he was dislodging an errant bug or eyelash. On second look I could see that his tears were streaming. He hugged his big sister and once again dried his eyes with the ready-made "handkerchief."

I saw a tall, strapping young man call out to another graduate of equal size. He raised both arms high above his head, part in triumph, part in invitation for a hug. They embraced each other like two powerful sumo wrestlers.

"We did it!" the graduate pronounced.

"We sure as hell did," said the other, lifting his friend off the ground.

I saw a pretty young lady who was a member of the small choir that sang during the program. I remembered her because I was touched by her struggle to keep her composure while singing. "Bless her heart," I had thought. As she walked past me, I smiled. At that moment I was full of emotion, an eye blink away from losing it. She must have sensed that. Without saying a word, she grinned and gave me a splendid hug, firm and honest.

"I almost broke up while watching you sing," I told her.

And then I did lose it. We stood there for a moment, face to face, total strangers and, yet, equal participants in the human experience. I did not know then, nor do I know now, the name of that mature young woman, but I thank her for taking me in.

Still I lingered. As I watched the crowd, I wished I could be everywhere all at once. I wanted to be sandwiched between every hug dispensed that night. I wanted to hear the words: the congratulations, the reconciliations, the remembrances, the dreams.

But soon, too soon, the crowd began to dwindle. Families returned to their homes, graduates found their parties, and I stood on the fifty-yard line of the high school football field and thought, "It does not get any better than that."

Those are the moments that make it all worth while —when the tears are dried and the battles forgotten. Only the spirit of each youth is important. The potential harnessed in those sturdy, young bodies is enough to power our dreams, heal the world, and move this 1964 high school graduate to tears of perfect joy.

ONE FRIDAY NIGHT AFTER WORK,
I drove home on a new stretch of freeway between
the place where I work and the place where I live.
I felt great. I was looking forward to dinner with
my wife and a game of tennis with a friend on
Saturday. I was feeling so good I began singing
about my plans for the weekend, beating out the
rhythm on the dashboard.

> *Well, I'm drivin' on home.*
> *Scoobie-shoobie doo.*
> *Gonna paint the town*
> *With my Sweet Baloo.*

I was working on the second verse when I
caught a glimpse of a woman in a BMW, tailgating
close enough to kiss me on the lips. I tried to get
out of her way, but I was flanked on both sides by
other cars. There we were, the four of us, looking
like the Blue Angles flying down the highway in a

perfect "T" formation. I looked in my rear view
mirror again. The lady did not look happy.

Finally, the car to my right pealed off at the
next exit. I faded over to the right lane, giving
the "Beamer" a clear lane to pass.

Then, just as the BMW pulled along side, I
turned my head to get a closer look at the driver.
I don't know why I looked. Maybe I wanted a peek
at raw impatience. Or maybe I just wanted to see
what a person rich enough to drive a BMW looks
like. So I looked.

What happened next caught me by surprise.
The woman cranked her head toward me, screwed
up her face like a dead cat on the freeway, placed
her right index finger to her temple, and twisted
her hand back and forth, the universal sign for that
philosophical question posed on all the streets and
highways in all the world: "ARE YOU WACKO OR
WHAT?"

Now, I don't think I had any control over my
first impulse; you know, that jolt of adrenaline that
squirts into your stomach. That was my defense
mechanism, my "fight or flight" impulse going into
action. That's natural; I had no power over that
instinctive, physiological response. But I did have

control over my thoughts and actions from that point on.

Frankly, I have to admit that my first thought was spiteful. "She's speeding, right? What if she were pulled over by the state patrol? Then when I drove by at 55 miles per hour in my '79 Honda Accord, I could give *her* the *Are-you-wacko-or-what?* sign."

And then I thought, "Hold on, you don't know this lady. She's a total stranger to you. What she thinks of you doesn't matter in the slightest. Are you going to let an impatient woman ruin a perfectly good weekend?"

The answer to that, of course, was "no." So I decided to take a different approach. I decided to use a popular behaviorist technique called "thought stopping." I use it whenever I want to dispose of mental garbage. It works like this.

1. As soon as I catch myself obsessing over a miserable thought, I shout "STOP!" At the same time, I give myself a little pinch on the wrist. Some people press their fingernails into the palm of their hands. Others will snap their wrists with a rubber

band "bracelet." Whatever the technique, it is not necessary to draw blood. The idea is merely to let the brain know that this "miserablizing" will not be tolerated.

2.   I immediately visualize something extremely pleasant. Use whatever works for you: skiing down a beautiful mountain slope or sunbathing on a deserted, tropical beach. I usually rely on a good sexual fantasy myself.

3.   If the miserable thought returns—and it usually does in about 10 to 15 seconds— I repeat steps one and two. After doing this a few times, I find that the negative thought eventually disappears altogether.

The beauty of this technique is that you can use it anywhere, even in a business meeting. Of course, you do draw attention to yourself if you suddenly belt out: "STOP!" People tend to wonder. But, with a little practice, the technique works just as well by saying, whispering, or even thinking "stop."

So I did the "thought stop," and it worked. I had a wonderful evening with my wife and a great tennis match the next morning. And I never once thought about the impatient woman in the BMW, except to write this piece. And for that, BMW Lady, I thank you, wherever you are.

THE PROFESSOR WAS SLOW and deliberate.
He was so pokey I used to take notes in calli-
graphy. But no one protested.

I looked around the table. There were ten of
us, all Ph.D. candidates. We had not been officially
accepted into the program, so we measured our
words carefully. It was a game. We imagined what
was in the professor's mind and then fed it back to
him like a church choir. Basically, we played the
role of adoring disciples.

But "adoring" was never one of my strong
points; I resisted and, as a result, was almost
drummed out of the program. It happened like this.

The professor was leading another "high-
voltage" discussion. I was drifting in and out of
sleep when he said something that nudged me into
consciousness.

"In group therapy," he said, "you must forbid

your clients from interacting outside the counseling sessions."

"I disagree," I heard myself say.

My classmates bowed their heads and started picking lint off their clothes.

"In fact, I think Carl Rogers would support my position." Then I told him why.

I thought quoting Carl Rogers was a good move. He is one of America's most respected psychologists —clearly an authority on the subject.

The professor quickly dismissed my argument; he seemed annoyed by the interruption. By then, the room temperature had jumped one or two seasons. My fellow students were starting to pick lint off each *other's* clothes. I let it go.

That evening, though, I began thinking about what had happened. I was sure that Dr. Rogers would have agreed with me. So I did something outrageous; I set up a tape recorder and telephoned the famous psychologist at his home in California. I couldn't believe it when he actually answered the phone; I recognized his voice from his instructional video tapes.

I told him how much I admired his work and then asked him to comment on the issue I had raised in class.

HE AGREED WITH ME. And I had it all on tape to prove it.

The next day in class I did something really dumb. I reviewed what had happened the day before and then played the tape. The entire class inhaled in unison.

The professor said nothing; he just stared at me with a closed half smile. Oh-oh. Suddenly, I felt like a balloon dancer at a revival tent meeting.

Two days later, the department head told me I was on probation. When I asked why, he said I was seen as argumentative and insensitive. I was crushed; I saw three years of work clipped like a toenail.

I didn't know what to do. Finally, the one person I trusted, my committee chair, advised me to apologize to all my professors.

"For what?" I asked. "For challenging a concept? Isn't that what university life is about? Grappling with ideas? Is there no room on earth for controversy?" Boy, was I eloquent.

Still, even as I spoke, I knew he was right. So I lowered my head, laced my fingers, and made the rounds, each time begging forgiveness for my arrogance. It was not easy, but I did it. From that point on, I was the ideal student: silent and compliant. Two weeks later I was reinstated.

I know now I made it hard on myself. I was politically naive. It had not occurred to me that people in power are often driven by a tremendous ego. To go against them is to risk retribution.

I stood on the first rung in a towering political system, devoid of power. I would achieve my goal only by conforming to the standards of the system, however unjust.

That knowledge turned on my stomach like a bad meatball. How unfair, I thought. Who made the professor emperor of the universe? What is wrong with expressing a divergent idea? I was so angry I made myself sick.

Slowly, though, I accepted the idea that I had entered an agreement. It was not personal; it was a business deal. I exchanged my money and my compliance for a degree. I still retained my ideas. I still believed what I believed; no business transaction could take that away. I had only made a bargain. Understanding that made life easier — not jubilant, just easier — and for the time, that was good enough.

OKAY, I ADMIT IT, I'm losing my hair—
which is a funny thing to say. I mean, it's not like
I misplaced it somewhere.

"Sugar Cakes, have you seen my hair anywhere?"

"I don't know, Honey. Have you checked the
junk drawer?"

No, I'm not really *losing* it; it's just kind of
disappearing. Maybe the Hair Fairy comes in the
middle of the night when I'm asleep and harvests a
few strands at a time; I don't know. I do know
that it has been going on for some time. I'm not
totally bald yet, but I may be by next Tuesday.

Now, when you first wake up to this cruel trick
of nature, you begin doing funny things. You look
in the mirror and consider new and creative ways
to part your hair. Maybe you could crease it on
the side—you know, just above the left ear—

and sweep it across the top of your skull like a thatch of ivy. Or how about cutting a line straight down the middle like Dagwood Bumstead. Or what if you shaved it all off and grew a goatee and wore sunglasses a lot? People might not think of you as bald, just Bohemian.

When you're losing your fur, you start to move funny in a room. You always keep your back to the wall and stand tall so that no one can see the inverted saucer on the crown of your head. You never walk directly to the door to leave a room. You edge around the outside walls, shuffling your feet sideways—step, pull together, step, pull together. When you're bald, you have to allow for a lot of time to get from one side of the room to the other.

What a terrible condition: to face the world with more shine than twine, the curse of a leper chromosome.

But is it really so bad?

Sure, I now buff what I once fluffed, but it's not the end of the world. I still speak intelligible English. I still have a few friends—some of them with full heads of hair. I still manage to eke out a living. I am not ready to give it all up and ride the rails.

"Yep, I was a successful businessman back in
'90, but then I lost my hair, and I began to fall so
low."

[A woeful harmonica is heard off stage.]

> *Ain't got no cause for livin'*
> *That is plain to see.*
> *Cause when I went to Memphis*
> *My hair went to Orleans.*

"I lost my job, my family, everything. I knew
I hit rock bottom when I broke into my kid's piggy
bank to support my habit for baseball caps."

No, it's not that bad. We are all born with a
collection of gifts and practical jokes. That is the
way it is; no sense complaining about it. If you
don't like it, devise another system. Meanwhile, it
seems to me that what makes most sense is to
accept who I am, the way I am.

My wife has taught me that in her own playful
way. She sustains a running joke about the other
end of me: my toes. My wife's toes are praise-
worthy, small and regular, descending in size in an
orderly manner. "They are the way toes are
supposed to be," she says.

On the other hand—er, foot—my toes are

bulky, irregular, and descend in a random, free-spirited order. Whenever I take my socks off at the end of the day, my wife makes some kind of snide comment.

"Yipes, the toes that devoured Manhattan. Quick, cover them up before they go berserk!"

She never makes any sense, but I hide them anyway, feeling like Lon Chaney as the misunderstood werewolf. "I'm really a nice person, once you get to know me."

Of course, my wife's teasing is her way of saying that we are both perfectly all right the way we are — I with my glossy dome and she with her designer toes, which is exactly how it should be.

There is no sense agonizing over those physical characteristics which are outside my control — the family nose, the inherited love handles, the size thirteen gondolas. What I *can* zero in on are my destructive habits, compulsive thoughts, and irrational behaviors. Those are the states I have the power to alter. And that is where my energy should be directed — toward the things I *can* change.

Sure, my hair has taken an extended leave of absence and, yes, my toes compose an admittedly ragged skyline, but that's okay. No sense worrying about what other people think. Most likely, they're not thinking about me anyway; they're worrying about what I'm thinking about them.

WHEN I WAS A JUNIOR IN COLLEGE, I began wishing my life away. Enough, already, with French and philosophy and Principles of Education; I wanted a real job. I wanted to be in the classroom—exploring the great ideas and molding young, enthusiastic minds. I pictured myself a young Glenn Ford, turning the blackboard jungle into a serene, loving, educational commune ——a kind of Woodstock with clothes.

That all changed the first day of my teaching career. In the first few minutes of the first period, I met a 16-year-old boy who sported a T-shirt with a caricature of a naked lady and the caption "Stronger Than Beer." He sat in the front seat of the middle row, his legs extended and crossed at the ankles, the pointed soles of his cowboy boots bellied-up. He looked as if he slept maybe once every three days.

Suddenly, I had the sickening feeling that I had
made a horrible mistake. What did I know about
teaching anyway? Maybe I was meant to be a
doctor or a lawyer or . . . a shepherd. Maybe, on
the day I was born, my name tag was switched with
another kid, and I should really be a cosmopolitan
playboy. Yeah, that must be it. Surely, I was not
destined to suffer through 120 sophomore themes
over a meat loaf and tatertots TV dinner.

That experience was a revelation. I suddenly
realized that I had been acting as though life were
a destination. It is not, of course; it is a journey.

Somehow, I had forgotten that. For four years,
I had focused all my energy on becoming a teacher.
When the day finally arrived, I stopped, looked
around, and — like Peggy Lee — asked, "Is that
all there is?" I expected nirvana; instead I
discovered troubled kids and a cold, standup
radiator that clanked in the winter. I felt empty
and disillusioned.

At that moment I was on the far side of crazy.
The problem, though, was not with the school or
with the kids; it was with me. I had the idea that
life should be orderly and predictable — kind of
like fast food or half-hour doses of sitcom

television. I expected everything to be pat and comfortable —a pleasant destination; then I would be happy.

I was wrong. I'm persuaded now that the best times are when I live on the edge, gently nudged out of my comfort zone. That is when I feel most alive, when I can experience —and relish—the tension of the journey.

That first day at school was not the last day of my teaching career. I was determined to make something happen in the classroom, to act as a learning "travel agent."

So I pushed against the envelope of my comfort zone is small ways: reading Edgar Allan Poe by candlelight, holding a trial on the quality of education, staging a fight with a student to kick off a lesson on conflict. My goal was to make learning as experiential as possible. My ideas did not always work, but I had a hellava good time.

I was learning to embrace the uncertain adventures in my life: the tension of a new idea, the ambivalence of a rare sensation, the misgivings of confrontation. I was learning to enjoy the journey and to yearn for the road not yet taken.

THE SUBTITLE OF THIS BOOK is *Lessons On Living From Someone Who Should Know Better But Keeps Messing Up Anyway.* At first the line was written for a laugh. But now, at the end of the book, I find that there is more truth than folly in the words. I *should* know better. My only comfort is that the telling of each story may awaken my senses and keep me on this side of crazy.

So, one final story to help me help myself:

It was the opening game of the season. I was coaching first base, and my wife was up to bat. The count was 3 and 0. The pitcher began his windup. My wife leaned over the plate, her bat resting demurely on her right shoulder.

"Take it!" I shouted.

The ball skittered through the air; it looked like a sure walk. Incredibly, though, my wife cocked her bat and swung. The ball dribbled off her timber and rolled half way to the pitcher's mound: an easy out.

"Why did you swing?" I demanded.

"You told me to," she snapped back.

"I told you to take it."

"I DID TAKE IT!"

Oh.

ABOUT THE AUTHOR

Besides being a writer, Allen Johnson is a professional speaker, trainer, and organizational consultant — his work founded on a Masters in speech and a Ph.D. in Counseling Psychology.

In his life he has been a college professor in Oregon, a language teacher in North Africa, an entertainer on Catalina Island.

Through his professional speaking and consulting firm, Johnson Dynamics, he conducts seminars on "Managing Relationships" and "Building Teams." As an organizational consultant, he facilitates positive change through systems analysis, problem solving, goal setting, and team building.

Finally, as a keynote and banquet speaker — tagged *The Standup Doctor* — he is in demand in half the United States . . . and *wanted* in the other half.

SERVICES & PRODUCTS BY ALLEN JOHNSON

Allen Johnson is available for keynote and banquet presentations, seminars, and organizational consulting. Address inquiries to *Renaissance Publishing House* as shown below.

Audio Cassette Albums

This Side of Crazy

The author reads his insightful, heart-warming stories in this attractive, unabridged four-cassette album. Running time: 3 hours, 33 minutes. ISBN 0-9626600-1-9. $39.95 (WA tax $3.12.)

Love, Power, and the Freedom to Be

Four 60-minute audio cassettes. Allen Johnson offers dynamic models for understanding motivation, goal setting, conflict resolution, and the need for approval. $39.95 (WA tax $3.12.)

This Side of Crazy (the book)

Additional copies of Allen Johnson's book, *This Side of Crazy*, may be ordered directly from *Renaissance Publishing House*. ISBN 0-9626600-0-0. $9.95 (WA tax 78 cents.)

Include $2.00 for shipping and handling for the first item and $.75 for each additional item. Washington Residents add 7.8% sales tax. Visa and Master Card accepted. (Include credit card name, number, and expiration date.) Inquire about volume discounts. Mail to:

Renaissance Publishing House
2618 Quarterhorse Way
Richland, WA 99352
(509) 627-3000